Our Gohman Story

Our Gohman Story
The First and Second Generations

Roy Evans
& Charlie Kunkel

authorHOUSE®

AuthorHouse™
1663 Liberty Drive
Bloomington, IN 47403
www.authorhouse.com
Phone: 1 (800) 839-8640

Published by AuthorHouse 04/10/2015

ISBN: 978-1-5049-0520-6 (sc)
ISBN: 978-1-5049-0519-0 (e)

Library of Congress Control Number: 2015905721

Print information available on the last page.

*Any people depicted in stock imagery provided by Thinkstock are models,
and such images are being used for illustrative purposes only.
Certain stock imagery © Thinkstock.*

This book is printed on acid-free paper.

CONTENTS

REMEMBERING FR. CHARLIE

Fr. Charles "Charlie" William Kunkel, O.S.C.

Fr. Charles "Charlie" William Kunkel, O.S.C. was a fifth-generation Gohman. He was born November 16, 1940, to Vincent and Leona (Potthoff) Kunkel in Pearl Lake, Stearns County, Minnesota. He died October 12, 2014, in Onamia, Milaca County, Minnesota.

Fr. Charlie attended the Crosiers' Seminary in Onamia from 1954 until 1960. He joined the Crosiers as a novice and was vested in the Crosier habit on August 27th, 1960, in Hastings, Adams County, Nebraska and made his first profession of vows there on August 28, 1961. He earned his bachelor's degree at St. Francis College and his theology degree from the Crosier House of Studies, both in Fort Wayne, Allen County, Indiana. He was ordained a Crosier priest on June 3, 1967, in Fort Wayne.

His ministry assignments included service on the faculty of the Crosiers' Wawasee Preparatory School in Indiana; leadership as Prior in the Crosier communities of Fort Wayne, Phoenix, and Hastings; and service as Pastor at St. Odilia Church in Shoreview, Minnesota and St. Mary's Church in Milaca, Minnesota. His last assignment was as Novice Director for the Crosiers until cancer made this impossible during July 2014.

Fr. Charlie's avocation was writing and the study of genealogy, especially the study of Gohman and Kunkel families. Under his leadership and personal research, knowledge about the Gohman family was vastly expanded. He was the author of "Raising Roger's Cross" and co-author of two genealogy books, the two volumes of "Our Gohman Story".

Our Ancestors

We know their names now,
Our ancestors,
Their dates and ages,
Their births and dying's,
Their love of family and children,
And their long journeys
Away from home
To seek a new place to live.

We wonder now about their hearts,
Our ancestors,
Their longings that drove them,
Their dreams that quieted them,
Their heartaches that worried them,
And their long journeys
Away from home
To seek a new place to live.

We are more amazed about them now,
Our ancestors,
Their pioneer spirit and tenacity,
Their resilient grit to grow things,
Their joy in creating big families
And their long journeys
Away from home
To seek a new place to live.

We love them now as they loved us,
Our ancestors.
We thank them for believing in God.
We thank them for giving us life.
We thank them for their sacrifices.
And we thank them, most of all,
For taking their long journeys
Away from home
To seek a new place for all of us to live.

-- Charlie Kunkel --

ACKNOWLEDGEMENTS

The research behind this volume of "Our Gohman Story" is the result of the collaboration and efforts of many Gohman cousins, their spouses, and friends. Working under the tutelage and leadership of Fr. Charlie Kunkel; Tim Ahles, Ben Carlson, Roy Evans, Wayne Fandel and Terry Machtemes made major contributions in time and effort. Fr. Charlie's personal efforts were supported, in a significant way, by the work of Alan Bernard in Cincinnati and Andy and Liz Woebkenberg in Germany.

A special thanks to Terry Machtemes and Ben Carlson. Terry Machtemes did the translation of numerous early documents and other records that were originally written in the German language. He also was the resident Canadian researcher. Ben Carlson clarified the many puzzles related to the Gohman homesteads and made an understanding of their history possible. The extensive and highly detailed appendix "Gohmans and the Land" was researched and prepared by him.

Background images for the Gohman Land appendix maps were produced by the National Agriculture Imagery Program (NAIP) and published by the Aerial Photography Field Office (AFPO), both of which are administered by the USDA's Farm Service Agency (FSA).

The "Our Ancestors" poem plus the "Finding the Gohman Family" appendix, and the "Charlie's Other Research and Thoughts" appendix were authored by Fr. Charlie Kunkel. He also authored the first four and one half chapters of the book with edits by Roy Evans.

The book cover design was taken from Fr. Charlie's design for the cover of the earlier volume with permission to use the scenic photo taken by Ben Carlson. The new ghost images were selected and prepared by Roy Evans.

The remaining sixteen chapters of the book and three appendices content were authored by Roy Evans including all the image selection and preparation.

Lastly and critically important, the book manuscript received a final review and edit by fifth generation Gohmann, Kathy Evans.

AUTHORS

The co-author, LeRoy (Roy) Evans was born and raised in central Minnesota and currently lives in eastern North Carolina. He had the good fortune of marrying a Gohmann descendant in Minnesota. Twice retired; first from the United States Marine Corps and then from a not-for-profit corporation, his current interests include genealogy and computers.

The co-author, Fr. Charlie Kunkel, O.S.C., was born and raised in central Minnesota and lived in the Crosier Priory at Onamia, Minnesota until his death October 12, 2014. His great-grandfather was one of the second-generation Gohman descendants featured in this book. In addition to his life and work as a Crosier and a priest, he enjoyed genealogical research and creative writing.

Captivated

by the

Gohman Story
(Revisited)

Two itinerant men wander into two German towns in close proximity but some 50 years apart. From those men came two descendants, a man and a woman, that eventually meet. After traveling nearly a fourth of the way around the world, the couple wed in a new land and become the patriarch and matriarch of an amazing Gohman family and subject of the two volumes of "Our Gohman Story".

One author of the book was told, "Do not even try to write the history of the Gohman family. It is too large and too complicated. You will never be able to figure it out". The challenge was so great and the reward so meaningful that a small group of Gohman cousins and spouses decided it could be done, resulting in the two volumes.

It became necessary to adopt common terminology for organizing and explaining the data concerning this huge family:

> *The original individuals who immigrated to the United States, Johann Diedrich Gohmann and Marie Elisabeth Börger, are known as the first-generation or immigrant generation ancestors. They are also known as the patriarch and matriarch of this Gohman family. Their nine children are the second-generation and their grandchildren are the third generation.*

> *During the period this book covers, the general area the Gohman and Börger families originated from was in constant political upheaval. As a result, many names were used to identify it; Holy Roman Empire, Prussia, Hanover, Oldenburg, and others. The*

decision was made to simply call it by its current name, Germany, unless necessary to clarify a fact or event.

Given and Surname usage was also standardized and will be explained later in the book as individuals are introduced.

Many use the terms emigrant and immigrant interchangeably but it was decided to use the two terms according to their published definitions. Emigration is the act of leaving a country for another. Immigration is the act of arriving in a country from another.

Our Gohman Story started many centuries ago in a place still unknown. In the late 1700s the father of the family's patriarch, known as Diedrich Gohmann, migrated from an unknown location to Ankum, Germany. There, he and his family lived for two generations. The matriarch's family lived for many generations in the area of Damme, Germany, only a short distance from Ankum. In the mid-1840s the patriarch and matriarch of this Gohman family immigrated to Cincinnati, Ohio, where they married, had nine children, subsequently 65 grandchildren, and launched the large extended Gohman family that we know today.

The first published volume of *Our Gohman Story* was subtitled *The Third Generation*. In it, Gohman Cousins researched records, found living descendants if possible, and gradually discovered the unique story of each ancestor belonging to the third generation of the Gohman family. As the understanding of these ancestors grew, so did respect for each of them and for their special contribution to the Gohman history and story. The volume was published first at the urging of fourth-generation elders.

This volume of *Our Gohman Story*, the second, is subtitled "*The First and Second Generations*". It tells the earlier story of the Gohman origins plus that of the first, the immigrant generation, and second-generation ancestors. Hopefully others will take up the challenge in the future and tell the story of the fourth-generation ancestors.

Gohman Ancestors Called Into the Light

Like most pioneer people, the early Gohman family did not dwell on the past but put their efforts toward building a new life in a new land. They had little time to look back and ponder where they had come from. Johann Diedrich and Marie Elisabeth firmly instilled this culture in their children. It was adhered to, more or less, by the second, third and fourth generations of the Gohman family. Only the fifth-generation descendants were inclined to look back and ask who these ancestors were, what did they experience in life and what can we learn from them? Government and church record keeping was at an infancy throughout the immigrant and second generation era and related documents and records were often not available. Telling the Gohman family story became a difficult task.

Nonetheless, it was possible to write an interesting history of the family and two volumes of *"Our Gohman Story"* resulted. Even those family members who died at an early age were given their rightful place within the family and give a story of their own. A diligent effort was made to discover the unique contribution of each person. In writing the history and the story of each married second generation ancestor, the spouse was recognized as an important partner in the overall development of the Gohman family. Their family stories are included as sub chapters throughout this volume.

In the first volume of *Our Gohman Story*, the reader was encouraged to read, first of all, the story of their own third-generation ancestor. After absorbing that special story, they were encouraged to go on to study the other stories and appendices as well. In this volume, the reader is advised to read the entire family history leading up to the individual second generation stories. After that, read the story about the second generation ancestor of interest, and then complete the book by reading the remaining stories and appendices.

Legacy of the Gohman Family Name

This information was first presented in the first volume of *"Our Gohman Story"* but is repeated here for clarification of this volume.

In many old records the Gohmañ name was spelled with a tilde over the letter "n." The tilde is sometimes called a "squiggly," which in this case indicates a missing letter, namely a second "n." Thus Gohmañ is the same as Gohmann.

The last name of our patriarch, Johann Diedrich Gohmann, was spelled in various ways on records in Germany; Cincinnati, Ohio; and St. Augusta, Minnesota. It was spelled as Gohmañ, Gohmann, Gomañ, Gomann, and Gohman. However the predominant spelling of the original name used two "nn" or one "ñ" with the tilde.

Some family branches and family groups kept the spelling of Gohmann with two nn's; others decided to spell Gohman with one "n." Thus closely related cousins in the extended family have the same name but it is spelled differently. Other pioneer families have experienced similar name modifications. However this spelling change created a challenge in writing the history of these ancestors. It was decided to use the spelling that each family group chose for itself, knowing that some mistakes invariably would be made. Also it was decided to use the shorter form, Gohman, in the title of the volumes and for other uses of the name not directly related to one of the family groups. None of the stories about the family name could be verified, nor could any one of them explain the whole story about how the spelling of the family name changed. It is simply a fact of

3

Gohman family history that some members of the family spelled their name with two "nn's" and some spelled it with one "n."

Gohman Love for the Mississippi

Some of this information was first presented in the first volume of *"Our Gohman Story"* but is, in part, repeated here, in an edited and condensed version.

The Mississippi River was a good friend to the Gohman family. Sometimes it could be a challenging friend, even a foe. Johann Diedrich Gohmann, the family patriarch, came to central Minnesota from Cincinnati, Ohio. Traveling on the river with his family, Diedrich discovered how challenging and unforgiving the river could be.

Diedrich settled on the western bank of the Mississippi on alluvial land, often called river bottomlands. Such land was exceptionally fertile and capable of bountiful harvests. As the Gohman family discovered, the fertility was the result of new soil deposited by large floods which occurred periodically. Diedrich's children followed in his footsteps when they began their own homes and farms by acquiring land as close to the Mississippi as possible. The mighty river was magnet that held the Gohmans together. The original homestead of the patriarch and matriarch was 0.13 miles (236.4 yards) from the river on the west bank. The homestead of John Bernard "Barney" Gohman and Katherine "Kate" Mund was 2.1 miles (3687.3 yards) west of the river. The homestead of Anna Maria Agnes Gohmann and Henry John Berger was immediately south of the patriarch's homestead and was 0.31 miles (540.9 yards) from the river on the west bank. George Henry Gohmann and Elizabeth Witschen homesteaded 1.1 miles (1938.3 yards) west of the river. John Diedrich Gohman and Mary Gahr first purchased the patriarch's homestead west of the river but then they purchased a much larger farm on the east bank with their home built about 100 feet from the river; this homestead was 9 miles south of St. Cloud and 3.5 north of Clear Lake. The homestead of Joseph Gohmann and Rose Marie Koenig was 4.35 miles (7652.7 yards) east of the river, east of Clear Lake. Anna Maria Elizabeth Gohmann and Anton Gambrino lived in the City of St. Cloud with their first home about 1.5 miles west of the river and later 0.88 miles (1546.3 yards) west of the river. Finally Stephen Gohmann and Catherine "Kate" Wamka started farming near Joseph Gohmann and the distance would also have been about 4.35 miles east of the river.

Life Span of First and Second Generation Gohmans

Some of this information was first presented in the first volume of *"Our Gohman Story"* but is repeated here, in a version edited and expanded to include information emphasizing the first and second generations.

The children and grandchildren of Johann Diedrich Gohmann and Marie Elisabeth Börger had a strong and healthy start in life. Seven of their nine children survived into maturity, married and had families, an important and promising family trait. These seven children of the second generation had a total of sixty-five children.

The lives of Johann Diedrich and Marie Elisabeth Gohmann and their children spanned the years 1814 to 1946, an amazing span of 132 Years. The second generation, alone, spanned the years 1847 to 1946, an equally amazing 99 years. During that era many historic and often dramatic events helped to shape their character, their family and their lives.

Many of the historically significant events during the lives of the first or immigrant and second generation are chronicled in their stories to follow. Some additional Minnesota historically significant events that occurred during their lives are summarized here.

The Gohman family was part of an 1853-1857 population explosion that occurred in the Minnesota Territory when it grew from 40,000 people to approximately 150,000 people. They first arrived in the new city of St. Paul which had incorporated as a city in 1854. It covered an area of about four square miles.

Diedrich may have joined the other residents of the Minnesota Territory in ratifying a proposed state constitution during 1857. That year, a financial panic sent prices skyrocketing; banks and businesses failed, and the resulting financial depression lasted until 1861.

During 1858, widespread newspaper promotion of the Minnesota Territory brought large numbers of new settlers and over one thousand steamboats arrived in St. Paul. May 11, 1858, Minnesota became the thirty-second state admitted to the union of the United States.

In 1861, a civil war broke out in the United States. Initially, Minnesota sent 1,000 volunteers for service in the Union Army. It eventually provided 24,000 men for fighting in the Civil War and, in 1862, an Indian conflict.

New markets for the Gohman farm crops and animals became available when a railroad was completed in 1862 that connected Minneapolis and St. Paul with eastern cities. By April 1866, the railroad connected St. Cloud with the cities of St. Paul and Minneapolis. By October of the same year, two trains a day were arriving and departing St. Cloud.

During the 1863 Battle of Gettysburg, the First Minnesota Regiment made a heroic charge and lost 215 of its 262 men. April 13, 1865, news was spread throughout the St. Augusta area that General Lee's army had surrendered and the Civil War was over. The Gohman family and their neighbors were greatly relieved. A short time later, April 20, 1865, they were saddened to hear the report of President Lincoln's assassination. Nearby St. Cloud declared a time of mourning and suspended business the day of his funeral. Stearns County with only a population of 3,881 men provided 688 soldiers during the war.

January 1873, a three day long snow storm hit Minnesota and some seventy Minnesotans were killed. The Gohman family, then, had to fight a natural scourge. From 1873 to 1877 hordes of grasshoppers invaded Minnesota farms, devouring everything in their paths. The Gohman farms in central Minnesota were damaged less than those in southwestern regions of the state. Farm production and income was still reduced significantly. Many farmers abandoned their farms but the Gohman families persevered.

By 1880 wheat farming became the primary money maker for the Midwestern farmer and Minneapolis, Hennepin County, Minnesota was the flour-milling capital of the United States. Growing wheat quickly depleted the soil's nutrients. The Gohman farmer's river bottom soil lasted longer than most but the depletion was a problem nonetheless. Farmers had to learn to rotate their crops, switch to producing hogs and/or beef cows, or they had to move on to fresh soil. A look at the history of the Gohman families will show that the second-generation diversified their farming but some of the third-generation began to move around.

In 1889 the Russian Influenza pandemic circled the globe in just four months. It led to a summer of diarrhea and dysentery for children around the world, including central Minnesota. As a result the United States published the Infectious Disease Notification Act of 1889, the first law of its kind in the United States. Like their neighbors, the Gohman family experienced the pain and suffering resulting from the death of members of the second generation and some of the newly born grandchildren.

The Model T became commonly available in 1908. It was the harbinger of change from horse and buggy to the automobile. With the introduction of this motor vehicle, tractors also began to appear in the farmer's fields. The Sunday trip to the local Catholic Church became more feasible as the Gohman family slowly adopted this new means of transportation. The second-generation watched as the third-generation took the new mechanization and adapted it to other farm support uses such as saw mills and powering of a paddlewheel boat.

Another influenza pandemic brought havoc to the world from 1918 to 1920. It was commonly known as the "Spanish Flu." Again, it did not spare the people of central Minnesota. Most victims were healthy young adults in contrast to most previous influenza outbreaks that predominantly affected young children and the aged. The Gohman family was tried and tested as they endured the traumatic effects of the flu and loss of a number of their loved ones. Many families in central Minnesota were almost wiped out by this virulent disease. The strength of the Gohman family was apparent as they weathered this onslaught.

World War I, or the "Great War" as it was known, was a war that was centered in Europe but affected the entire world. The war started on July 28, 1914, and lasted until November 11, 1918. During the war there were three registrations for the draft; June 5, 1917, June 5, 1918, and September 12, 1918. Each of the draft registrations were periods of deep concern to the Gohman family as many of their men were in the designated age groups. As it turned out, their food production as farmers was considered more important to the nation than their ability to fight. A few also received medical deferments due to earlier injuries or medical problems.

The 1920s brought a boom period of speculation both in investments and in farm production. Like the other farmers along the entire length of the banks of the Mississippi, the Gohman families expanded their land holdings, purchased modern machinery and dramatically increased their farm crop production. Mother Nature was supportive and each year the Gohman farmers had bumper crops. During the early part of 1929, the enormous overproduction of grain, especially wheat, drove the prices to almost zero. Throughout the early part of the year, the prices fluctuated wildly. As fall approached and another bumper harvest was ready to sell, many attempts were made to stabilize the market. By October 1929, falling commodity markets in the United States and other countries around the world shook investor self-confidence and the stock market started to feel the effects. On October 24, panic selling began in the stock market, and the Wall Street Crash of 1929 became reality. The Gohman farmers found themselves with mouths to feed, bills to pay, and no market for their crops in the field ready for harvesting. With the banks failing, the Gohman families lost what little cash they had and nowhere to borrow more. The Crash was the beginning of a period when the Gohman family once again would have the strength of its character tested.

The Crash began what is known as the Great Depression. History books usually report that it lasted from 1930 to about 1940. The Great Depression combined with a severe drought on the Great Plains during the years 1931 - 1936 made farming next to impossible. Thousands of families were displaced from their farms but the Gohman families were determined to tough it out. Living literally from "hand to mouth," the family gardens kept them sustained. Scavenged greens and wild berries from along the banks of the Mississippi added to their diet. Butchering and consuming the meat from the family farm animals was limited as they could not afford to replace the animals. In reality they had become subsistence farmers. During the boom years of the '20s some of the Gohman families had borrowed heavily. They were now facing farm foreclosures and bankruptcy. Several lost their farms and either rented another or went looking for other work. The Gohmans were a shrewd bunch and using the bankruptcy laws of the day, some figured out a way to preserve the family farm. Farms were signed over to large corporations, financial organizations and even some large public entities and the families remained on the farms as caretakers. By 1932, with the Depression worsening, the Minnesota legislature proposed low-interest farm loans and a state unemployment insurance program. The progressive 1933 legislature created a moratorium on mortgage foreclosures and a reduction in property taxes for farmers. Gohman families took advantage of these tools. After the economy turned around, many of the farms that had been turned over to others were returned to their original owners with few, if any, obligations.

In 1935 electrification came to rural Minnesota. Initially the Gohman families could not afford to take advantage of this new miracle. As the Depression lessened and farm income improved, they began to adopt the new farm tools and home comforts that electricity made possible.

7

The United States effort to support its allies and its own preparation for World War II finally brought the depression to an end. The war lasted from 1935 to 1945 with the United States formally entering the war in 1941. By then the children of the second-generation were too old to enlist or be drafted. However the second-generation as a whole felt the effects of the war through their farming contributions to the war effort and through their children and grandchildren. The younger third-generation men were deferred from the draft because of their employment in agriculture. Several large plants for manufacturing the materials of war were built in the Minneapolis – St. Paul area. A huge government arsenal for the manufacture of armaments followed. The second-generation watched as some of the Gohman families temporarily relocated to work in those plants and arsenal. The remainder stayed on their farms and increased production of food for the war effort. Although deferred from the draft because of their work in agriculture, many of the third-generation sons and even their daughters wanted to do more. During the course of the war, many joined the armed forces and served in all branches of service. One of the Gohman boys was killed test-flying a captured German aircraft. Others served heroically and participated in some of the turning points of the war.

The second generation grew to adulthood and old age, experiencing a lot of hard work, sometimes great deprivation and persistent change as a way of life. As children they spent their days working alongside their parents on the farm adjacent to the Mississippi River. As adults they continued to live near the river in homes without electricity or indoor plumbing. They attended one-room schools when they could, often walking long distances to get there. Transportation, when available, was by horse and farm cart or maybe a buggy. When there was a little time for play, they made their own fun.

German Origins

Gohman Family Origins

This Central Minnesota Gohman family came from Ankum in northwestern Germany. Ankum is located in the district of Osnabrück which is in the state of Niedersachsen, also known as Lower Saxony.

The Gohman family spoke the "Plattdeutsch", now known as "low German", dialect of the German language. That dialect was spoken primarily in northern Germany and the eastern part of the Netherlands. It is thought to have developed from a very early Saxon language. With the Plattdeutch dialect came ingrained traditions and a way of life that were different from the Germans who spoke the "Hochdeutsch" or "high German" dialect. The Hochdeutch dialect was spoken in central and the southern highlands of Germany and neighboring alpine countries. The "low German" dialect was not very standardized and was adapted to fit needs of the various communities that spoke it. On the other hand, "high German" dialect was consistent in the communities that spoke it. Initially "Hoch" was understood to mean from the high country but then became known as educated or cultural. Eventually those who spoke "high German" came to look down or hold in contempt those who spoke "low German". Later, the German emigrants carried the resulting differences with them as they moved to other lands.

The name of the Gohman patriarch who immigrated to the United States and established this family was Johann Diedrich Gohmann. His father's name was also Johann Diedrich Gohmann. For reasons that will become clear later, unlike the earlier third-generation volume which used the name Johan, this text will identify the patriarch as "Diedrich". His father will be called "Dirk." Over time and different places, the family used many surname variations. Two variations will primarily be used in this book, Gohmann and Gohman.

Dirk Gohmann, the father of the patriarch of the family in this book, was married twice. His first wife was Anna Catherine Konnermann. Their wedding was celebrated at St. Nicolaus Catholic

Church in Ankum, November 26, 1793. Four children were born from this first marriage. Catherine died on October 22, 1803 when she was 35 years old.

After Catherine's death, Dirk married Maria Alheid Schulte. She was commonly known by her second given name and in this book, Adelaid, which is the English version for Alheid, will be used. Their wedding was celebrated at St. Nicolaus Catholic Church, January 16, 1804. Five children were born from this second marriage, one of whom became the patriarch of this Central Minnesota Gohman Family.

The Ankum death record for Dirk indicates he died January 18, 1841, was 77 years old, and that he was a "husband from Tütingen." Tütingen was a farming area a few miles south of Ankum. The statement that he was a "husband from Tütingen" meant that his wife, Adelaid (Schulte) Gohmann, was still living at the time of his death. The fact that he was 77 years old at his death indicated that he was born about 1764. No record of his birth or baptism has been found in Ankum, which means that he was likely born elsewhere and migrated to Ankum. There is no known records that indicate where Dirk originated from.

Dirk Gohmann 1841 Ankum death record excerpt

Gohmann as Heuerlinger

Most likely Dirk Gohmann moved to Ankum to find work and support his family. Several church records reported that the Gohman family were Heuerlinger which were farm workers or tenant farmers. Patriarch, Diedrich Gohmann, also gave his occupation as a Heuerling on a list of emigrants who left Ankum in 1843 for the United States. Being a Heuerling meant that the Gohmann family were not property owners in Ankum but rather lived on other people's farms as laborers. They lived in special living quarters for the Heuerling, usually on the outer fringe of the farm, and away from the owner's personal home and farm buildings.

Heuerling home interior as is exhibited in the Cloppenburg Museum,
in the German town of the same name

Records indicate that the Gohmans lived and worked as Heuerlinger in Tütingen. The Tüting family had the largest farms in the area south of Ankum which resulted in the area being known as Tütingen. According to several Gohmann baptism records, members of the Tüting family occasionally served as a godparents for Gohmann children. A Tüting family member would never have served as a godparent for a Heuerling family from another farm. As a result, it is apparent that the Gohmann family lived and worked on the farms belonging to the Tüting family as Heuerlinger and that the two families had an unusually close relationship.

Motivation to Emigrate

Even before the Gohman family decided to join the emigration movement and leave Germany for the United States, they had been a family on the move. As Heuerlinger, they would have been looking for work on other people's farms. The family experienced relative stability during their 55 years in Ankum, but as Heuerlinger they understood that long-term stability was not to be expected. As a class, Heuerlinger were people on the move. As living conditions became more difficult and means of communication became more available, Heuerlinger became motivated by the dream of freedom. A dream of having their own land and to work for the prosperity of their own family. When emigration became a possibility, their dream of freedom could be developed into a plan.

Other reasons for emigration were shared by both property owners and Heuerlinger; all wanted to get out from under the overlords; the princes or prince-bishops who controlled large territories and taxed property and activities at every level of society. The owners of the Tüting farms, like other property owners, were held responsible for obligations to pay taxes to their overlords for almost anything that happened on their farms. For example, the birth of a child in their own family or in the family of their Heuerlinger could incur financial obligations to the overlord. The same thing was true of the birth of animal. Even a wedding or death of a farm associated family member resulted in a tax or fee for the farm owner. The amount owed was determined by the revenue needed by the prince or prince-bishop. Often the farm owner would use the work effort of his Heuerling servant and farm hands as a means of paying for these financial obligations. This kind of taxation and servitude increased the yearning to escape this social and economic bondage system.

Another motivation to emigrate resulted from the endless territorial wars. As a results of these conflicts, the overlords continuously drafted young men for their armies. Equally unsettling was the ongoing conflict between Catholic and Lutheran churches. The territorial conflicts often were tied to religious issues. Individuals and often whole communities were not free to practice their personal religion, but, had religion imposed on them by the overlord who controlled the land. This practice was known by the Latin phrase "Cuius regio, eius religio". The rulers of the German-speaking states and Charles V, Holy Roman Emperor, had agreed to the practice as early as 1555; ending a conflict between the Catholic and Protestant forces in the Holy Roman Empire.

Personal or family issues, also, often contributed to the dream for freedom. The German farming practices created a limited demand or capacity to employ the Heuerling. Young men often found no room for them or other available employment and they were forced to emigrate. Other young men wanted to avoid the army draft and would emigrate alone. Unmarried mothers were motivated to escape social stigma. Other young women hoped to find young men with whom to start a new life. Both often traveled alone or in arranged groups. Families who suffered the tragedy of the deaths of multiple children dreamed of a new life and would emigrate. Depressive and unchanging poverty afflicted many and helped create an undying dream for a better life and a reason to emigrate. Destitute people were often encouraged to emigrate by local authorities so that they would not become a burden to society. Occasionally, so many people left an area in a short period of time that officials did not register everyone one leaving. It was just too much paperwork.

Heuerling life in the early 19th century started as a need to survive but with a yearning to break free from it. That yearning grew into a plan to satisfy the dream of owning a farm and raising a family in freedom. This Gohmann family followed that path.

Börger Family Origins

Marie Elisabeth Börger married patriarch Johann Diedrich Gohmann in Cincinnati, Hamilton County, Ohio in 1845. In this text we will refer to Marie Elisabeth Börger as the matriarch.

Records indicate Marie Elisabeth Börger was commonly known by her second given name, "Elisabeth", and it also will be used in this book. The family surname was spelled as Börger or Boerger, not Berger or Burger. However, records include examples of the use of all these spellings. In this book the surname Börger will be used.

The Börger family came from northwestern Germany. They had lived in the farming area of Ihlendorf which is about 2 miles northeast of Damme, Germany. It is located in the district now known as Vechta and is in the state of Niedersachsen which is also known as Lower Saxony. Damme is about 15.5 miles northeast of the city of Vechta and about 13.5 miles east of Ankum.

In the Damme area, there were families of similar names; some were of the land owner class, known as Colons, and others were of the Heuerling class. According to church records, this Börger family belonged to the Heuerling class of farm workers in Damme at the same time that the Gohman family were Heuerlinger in Ankum. Some Börger family records included the abbreviation "He" to signify that Elisabeth's grandparents and parents on the Börger side were Heuerleute or Heuerling.

It is known that from 1675 to the 1840s, the Börger family lived in the area of Damme, including the neighboring villages of Ihlendorf, Sierhausen, Ossenbeck and Osterdamme. All these villages are only a few miles from the city of Damme. The Börger family experienced relative stability for a surprising amount of time in the Damme area.

The Börger family lived in the Damme area for at least seven generations until the 1840s when the Gohman matriarch, living siblings, and her father immigrated to the United States. Many other Börger family members also came to the United States while others continued to live in the Damme area.

Neighboring Cities; Ankum and Damme

Both Ankum and Damme are old cities, existing for 900 to 1000 years. The cities are relatively close neighbors, 13.5 miles apart, but with very different histories. However, during the period when the Börger family lived near Damme and when the Gohman family lived near Ankum, the citizens of the two cities commonly maintained business and social connections.

Records indicated that the Colons, that is, the farm owners from both cities often met about common interests. Many marriages between Colon families of these two areas took place. Also it was common for families from both areas to host matchmaking parties for unmarried individuals.

The two cities were within walking distance and Heuerling farm workers could readily travel back and forth. There is no record indicating that Diedrich Gohman and Elisabeth Börger met each other in Germany or knew each other's families before they immigrated to the United States. However, it is a very strong possibility.

In Damme and Ankum, as in many other German towns and farming areas, people began to plan, earn extra thalers or guilders (local silver and gold currency), sought out better options for themselves in far-away places, and even joined local city or church groups to organize emigration opportunities. Families often had to decide whether one or several persons should go first and get established or if all should go together. Emigration became a major force in German communities from the 1830s through the 1850s, especially in Damme and Ankum. In one day, 66 people left the neighboring town of Bersenbrück and immigrated to the United States. In Damme, the large emigration actually caused serious economic problems for the people left behind.

The City of Ankum

The first known record of the city of Ankum comes from the year 977. The city is located within a range of green wooded hills extending a long distance into Central Germany. Ankum is located on an ancient trail of megalithic or large stones stacked to create a man-made structure. The structures indicate that people lived in the area almost 5000 years ago.

In its earliest days, Ankum was a market place as it was an intersection of several trails. When roads replaced the trails, this crossing developed as a market place. While many things were being sold and traded, Ankum became known for being a cattle and horse market. The town began to develop as the animals needed feed plus places to be held and shown for sale. Sellers and buyers also needed places to reside on the marketing days. The town's tradition of providing lodging for the marketing public continues today as a tourist center. It is also still known as a leading market area for selling and buying horses.

The market in Ankum also offered the Heuerling farm workers the opportunity to look for work with a new Colon or land owner. Heuerling families could bring items to the market to sell. Most Heuerling families obtained raw harvested flax and during the winter months they would use it to weave linen fabric to sell. At the market, Heuerling workers could meet and organize work trips into the Netherlands during the German farming off-season. To earn some income, they would travel to the marshes along the Netherlands' North Sea coast. There they would cut blocks of peat to be dried and used as fireplace fuel. Often they worked in the cold wetlands in overcast rainy weather which resulted in many illnesses and loss of life. In addition to becoming a thriving market, Ankum became a place for the Heuerling to connect with others and look for ways to survive.

During the fifty years that the Gohman family lived in the Ankum area, they were members of the St. Nicolaus Catholic Church in Ankum. All of the family's baptism, marriage and death records from that church are found in the Osnabrück diocesan archives. The parish of St. Nicholaus has a long history, being established in the 1100s. For most of its history the Ankum parish was a parent parish for other smaller parishes in nearby villages. The oldest part of the church probably dates from as early as 1100 but it has been enlarged and rebuilt over the centuries. The main part of the current large church was built during the late 1800s and early 1900s.

The City of Ankum included several small surrounding communities; Ahausen-Sitter, Aslage, and Basum-Sussum. People living in Ankum proper were said to live in the Village of Ankum or the Ankum Parish. Several major farms were also nearby and included Lammerman, Starten, Wrocklaghink, Lager, and Tüting farms.

People from the various social classes worshipped together at St. Nicolaus Catholic Church. Heuerling families were expected to sit or stand in the back of the church while the Colon and other property owners occupied the front of the church. It was difficult for Heuerling workers to bathe and come to church in clean clothes like the farm owners and their families. Local tradition tells how the wealthy people had to walk past the Heuerling in church while attempting to ignore the odors the Heuerling brought from their farm work and living quarters. Heuerling children received little or no formal grammar school education but every parish had its own "Christenlehre" or "Sunday school" on Sunday afternoon. Most children in the St. Nicolaus parish received an introduction to the catechism and their Catholic faith.

St. Nicolaus Catholic Church, Ankum Germany

For several centuries the ordinary people of Ankum and surrounding area tolerated occasional changes in political/religious overlords. At times, the Lutheran Church provided the Prince Bishop and at other times the Prince Bishop was of the Catholic faith. These differences in

15

church authorities strengthened the people's personal religious convictions. In Ankum, there was a tradition for the local church leaders to work together regardless of who was in charge at the higher levels. There are examples in Germany of church buildings being occupied and record books maintained sometimes by Catholic clergy and sometimes by Lutheran clergy. Apparently even occasionally being shared by both clergies!

The City of Damme

The town of Damme was founded in 785 and about 800 the St. Victor Catholic Church was built. The tower of the current large church in Damme was built around 1100 on the ruins of an earlier Roman tower. The remainder of the church was built and remodeled over the years. Like the church in Ankum, the main part of the current St. Victor Catholic Church was built during the late 1800s and early 1900s.

St. Victor Catholic Church, Damme Germany

Damme was located at a pivotal geographical point between competing church and civil jurisdictions. During the thousand years from 800 to 1800, the area of Damme was constantly being exchanged between the dioceses of Osnabrück and Munster in negotiations after battles or other political conflicts. There was no other German region that experienced as many changes in church and civil boundaries as Damme. The ordinary people had to live with this lack of security as the will of the leaders of state and church were imposed on them. The farmers and other property owners bore significant political and financial burdens as the result of these changes. Some stability came to the area in 1803 when Damme became part of the Duchy of Oldenburg.

Ever since the early Middle Ages, Damme was a center of commerce and trade and the effects of its church and civil administration went far beyond its own city boundaries. Farming, weaving of linen, milling, harvesting peat and other commercial ventures made Damme an active business center. The city took pride in a tradition of having in its ranks construction masters who built the Fachwerkhaus homes and farm buildings that the area is famous for, even to this day. A Fachwerkhaus building was made of half-timber and half clay (loam) with straw fill that created a very attractive architectural design.

Fachwerkhaus home exhibit at the Cloppenburg Museum
in the town of the same name

A number of small surrounding communities were integral to the City of Damme. They included Borringhausen, Ihlendorf, Oldorf, Ossenbeck, Osterdamme, Osterfeine, Reselage, Rūschendorf, and Sierhausen. A number of major farms were also in the area and included Flöttel, Gers, Grever, Höltermann, Sanderman, Schröder, Wolke, and Börger. People coming from Damme proper, were said to have come from the Village of Damme.

Damme enjoyed an active social life and had numerous festivals. It was not uncommon for the farm owners and the Heuerling workers to socialize together. However this social life did not eliminate poverty and oppression as a huge and persistent problem for the Heuerling families of the Damme area. A higher than normal percentage of women could not bear children during this time because of malnutrition. Of the children that were born, many died before reaching adulthood. A common cause for death given on church records was malnutrition or emaciation. The Colon and Heuerling suffered together but the Heuerling being caught in the worst of the situation, experienced poor food, illness, weakness, inability to work, and often starvation.

Heuerling farm workers found hope for their families when emigration became a possibility.

17

Gohman Family in Germany

This begins the story of the Gohman Family journey and establishment of the family in a new land. Not all of the German part of the story can be documented. There are no surviving written stories, letters, photos or elder memories. Thankfully, there are valuable church records of baptisms, marriages and deaths and even a few immigration records. These records make it possible to reach back to the Gohman family in their homeland of Ankum, Germany and to understand something of their stories.

The patriarch's father, Dirk Gohmann, was born about 1764. The place of his birth and the names of his parents and possible siblings are not known. His birth year can be calculated, however, because his Ankum death record January 18, 1841 indicated that he died at the age of 77. He was married twice; first to Anna Catherine Konnermann and then to Maria Alheid (Adelaid) Schulte.

Dirk Gohmann and his first wife: Anna Catherine Konnermann

The Dirk and Anna Catherine Konnermann wedding was celebrated at St. Nicolaus Catholic Church in Ankum, November 26, 1793. Dirk was 29 years old and Catherine was 20 years old. Catherine was born March 25, 1773 in Ibbenbüren, Steinfurt, Nordrhein-Westfalen, Germany. Ankum and Ibbenbüren are about 30 miles apart. Catherine's parents were Johann Henrich Konermann and Maria Mollerherms. The marriage to Dirk Gohmann lasted for ten years from 1793 until Catherine's death in Ankum, October 22, 1803 when she was 35. Dirk and Catherine had four children, two sons and then two daughters.

Dirk and Catherine lived in a Heuerling house on the edge of the farm owned by the Tüting family a few miles south of Ankum. As a Heuerling house, it was probably poorly maintained and not a healthy place to raise a family. The walls and windows were likely drafty and did not protect the family from cold winds. They lived with an open fire pit that served for cooking and heating. When in use, it polluted the air in the house. Water for the family use had to be fetched from a distant cistern. Both Dirk and Catherine worked on the farm and the young children had to accompany them.

Dirk and Catherine Gohmann's four children were all born at home on the Tüting farm near Ankum and were baptized at St. Nicolaus Catholic Church.

Dirk and Catherine's first child: Herman Heinrich Gohmann

The first child of Dirk and Catherine Gohman was Herman Heinrich, born November 4, 1794. He was baptized November 12, 1794. His godparents are not known. It is likely that his two given names of "Herman" and "Heinrich" were connected to his baptism sponsors or uncles. As the oldest child, Herman cared for his younger siblings when his mother did her farm work or worked in her garden. Herman died on August 3, 1803 at the age of 8 years and 9 months. He was buried in Ankum on August 5, 1803. Herman's death was about 10 ½ weeks before his mother's death.

Dirk and Catherine's second child: Gerhard Heinrich Gohmann

Dirk and Catherine Gohmann's second child was another son, Gerhard Heinrich, born October 15, 1796. He was baptized October 18, 1796 and his Godfather was "Gerhard Heinrich G." who was most likely a Gohman and an uncle. Witnesses were Heinrich Von Hegel and Maria Aleid ("Adelaid") Schroe. Gerhard was seven years old when his mother died in 1803. As a young adult Gerhard worked on the Tüting farms. January 14, 1826, when he was 30 years old, Gerhard married Wilhelmina Catharina Josepha Rehe from Bersenbrück, which is about 3 ½ miles east of Ankum. The wedding took place at St. Nicolaus Catholic Church. The witnesses were Heinrich Heyen and Maria Gohman, most likely Gerhard's younger sister. Gerhard and Wilhelmina were blessed with a child, the first grandchild in Dirk's family, named Maria Elisabeth. She was born August 8, 1831 in Ankum and baptized at St. Nicolaus Catholic Church in Ankum August 10, 1831. On the child's baptism record Gerhard, the father, was listed as a "Tütingen," which meant that as an adult he had continued to work on the Tüting farms. He possibly had taken the place of his father as he aged and was unable to keep up the farm work. Gerhard was the first member of the Gohman family to immigrate to the United States, departing Bremen, Germany in 1834 when he was 38 years old.

Dirk and Catherine's third child: Maria Elisabeth Gohmann

The third child of Dirk and Catherine Gohmann was a daughter, Maria Elisabeth, born July 13, 1799. She was baptized July 16, 1799 and her godmother was Maria Elisabeth ____uberg (the surname on the record is not decipherable); witnesses were Herman Gramann and Maria Elisabeth Kloe. Maria Elisabeth was 3 years and 8 months old when her mother died. She lived in Ankum for about forty-five years and then most likely immigrated to the United States in 1845 with her half-sister, Anna Maria Elisabeth Gohmann. There is no record of her marriage or death in Ankum. There is, however, a record in Cincinnati, Hamilton County, Ohio of "Elisabeth Gohman" serving as godmother on April 5, 1847 for the baptism of John Bernard "Barney" Gohman, the oldest child of Diedrich Gohmann and Elisabeth Börger. No immigration, marriage or death record that can be specifically associated with Maria Elisabeth has been found in any Ankum, Cincinnati or other archives.

Dirk and Catherine's fourth child: Maria Adelaid Gohmann

Dirk and Catherine Gohmann's fourth child was Maria Aleid (Adelaid), born September 22, 1802. She was baptized September 23, 1802 at St. Nicolaus Catholic Church and her Godmother was Maria Adelaid Gohman, most likely an aunt. Two witnesses were Christina Tüting and Maria Elisabeth Konnermann Von Hegel. Christina Tüting would have been a member of the Tüting family which owned the farms on which the Gohman family lived and worked as Heuerling. This record further proves that the Gohman family was Heuerling on the Tüting farm and suggests that there was an unusually close relationship between these two families. Maria Adelaid had a short life, dying June 15, 1804 in Ankum at the age of 1 year and 9 months.

This was a very difficult time for the Gohman family, suffering three deaths within ten months from August 1803 to June 1804. The first child, Herman, died August 3, 1803. Two and one-half months later the children's mother, Anna Catherine, died October, 22, 1803. Eight months after the mother's death, her fourth child, Maria Adelaid, died June 15, 1804. The church records do not include a cause of death and one can only conjecture about the possible causes of death; poverty, poor living conditions, occasional epidemics or uncontrollable diseases.

Dirk Gohmann and his second wife: Maria Adelaid Schulte

Three months after his first wife died, Dirk Gohmann married Maria Alheid (Adelaid) Schulte, Monday, January 16, 1804. Their wedding was celebrated at St. Nicolaus Catholic Church and the witnesses were Anton Fiddeler and Heinrich Tarmelage. Anton Fiddeler was the sexton at St. Nicolaus Catholic Church and often served as a "fill in" proxy sponsor or witness for the Catholic ceremonies. Dirk was 40 years old when he married Adelaid and she was 22 years and 7 months old. She was born June 12, 1781 in Ankum to Gerhard Heinrich Schulte and Elisabeth Niemann. Dirk and Adelaid had five children, three sons and two daughters. One of their sons, Johann Diedrich, would become the patriarch of the large Gohman family in the United States.

Dirk and Adelaid Gohmann's five children were also born at home on the Tüting farm near Ankum. The parents continued the family tradition of having the children baptized at the St. Nicolaus Catholic Church.

Original St. Nicolaus Catholic Church baptismal font
used by the Gohmann family

Dirk and Adelaid's first child: Anna Maria Elisabeth Gohmann

The first child of Dirk and Adelaid was Anna Maria Elisabeth, born September 23, 1804. She was baptized September 26, 1804. The record, shown following, indicated her godmother was Anna Maria ___eimann (surname not fully decipherable); the witnesses were Johann Herman Heinrich Von Hegel and Maria Elisabeth Schulte.

Growing up as a Heuerling on the Tüting farms meant that Anna lived in poverty and had to work very hard. As a teenager and young adult she would have heard stories about the revolutions in France and in the United States and the rise of Napoleon. She would have experienced the growing desperation of Heuerling farm workers as they were cut off from other sources of extra income because of political unrest and economic changes. She would have been aware that it became more difficult to travel to Holland to harvest peat bogs and the markets for the domestically made linen were being overtaken by big producers.

It is likely in 1845, when she was 41 years old, Anna immigrated to the United States along with her half-sister, Maria Elisabeth. Either Anna Maria Elisabeth or her half-sister, Marie Elisabeth, served as the godmother for the child of the future patriarch and matriarch of the Gohman family in the United States. No emigration, immigration, marriage or death record that can be specifically associated with Anna Maria Elisabeth has been found in Ankum, Cincinnati, or any other possible location.

Dirk and Adelaid's second child: Johann Diedrich "Dirk" Gohmann

The next child of Dirk and Adelaid was Johann Diedrich "Dirk," born June 6, 1808. Johann Dirk was baptized on June 8, 1808. On his baptism record his father was listed as "zu Tütingen," which meant that he and his family were Heuerling workers on the Tüting farms. The godfather was Johann Dirk Ferber ("now Borgmann," according to the record). The witnesses were Johann Gerd (Gerhard) Bise and Maria Elisabeth Tüting. This last witness, who belonged to the Tüting family, indicated once again that at least one member of the Tüting family had a special relationship with the Gohman family. Johann Dirk lived for a short time. He died February 24, 1814 at the age of 5 years and 8 months.

Dirk and Adelaid's third child: Johann Heinrich Gohmann

The third child of Dirk and Adelaid was Johann Heinrich, born May 26, 1811. Johann Heinrich (known as "Heinrich" in Germany and as "Henry" in the United States) was baptized on May 30, 1811. Attached to his name on the baptism record are the words "ex Tütingen" verifying once again that his family were Heuerling workers for the Tüting farms. His godfather was Johann Heinrich _____ (surname not decipherable). The witnesses were Herman Schulte and Margaret Gertrud Hülschers.

When Heinrich was 30 years old, he married Maria Elisabeth (known as "Elisabeth") Barlage January 26, 1841 at St. Nicolaus Catholic Church. The witnesses at the wedding were Theodore Gohman (possibly his younger brother, Johann Diedrich) and Catherine Barlage. Elisabeth was 28 years old at the time of her wedding. She was born September 8, 1813 in Ankum. Her parents were Herman Heinrich Barlage and Maria Catharina Moller. Heinrich's father had died eight days before he and Elisabeth were married.

A list of Ankum emigrants indicated that Heinrich and Elisabeth left for the United States in 1845 and had been living in Westerholte, about 3 ½ miles south of Ankum. There is no record of any children born to Heinrich and Elisabeth during their four years of marriage in Germany.

Dirk and Adelaid's fourth child: Johann "Diedrich" Gohmann

The fourth child of Dirk and Adelaid was Johann Diedrich (known as "Diedrich"), born May 11, 1814. Diedrich was baptized May 15, 1814. His godfather was Johann Dirk _____; the witnesses were Johann Heinrich _____ and Maria Adelaid _____ (surnames cannot be deciphered).

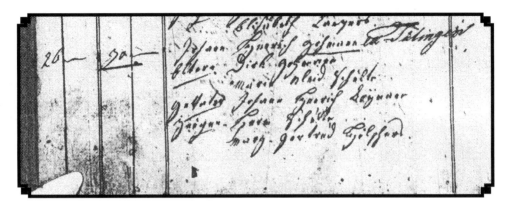

Johann Diedrich Gohmann baptism record excerpt

This son was born 45 days after his brother, Johann Diedrich, died and was given the same name. It was not an uncommon custom in those times to reuse the name of a sibling who has died. It would have been a comfort for the parents in their grief for the loss of the first child. As a teenager, Diedrich helped his parents on the Tüting farms and in the family's garden. As a young adult he searched out extra jobs for income to help support the family and to set aside for his future adventures. It is likely his social life included visits to Damme where he possibly met a special friend, Marie Elisabeth Börger, who was living with her family. In 1843 when he was 29 years old, Diedrich immigrated to the United States, where he became the patriarch of a large Gohman family and the subject of much of this book.

Dirk and Adelaid's fifth child: Maria Catherine Gohmann

The fifth and last child of Dirk and Adelaid was Maria Catharine, born November 5, 1817. Maria Catherine was baptized November 9, 1817 at St. Nicolaus Catholic Church. No baptism record was found for Maria Catharine but basic birth and death data was included on a family Index in the archives of the church. October 26, 1845, two weeks before her 28th birthday, Maria Catherine married Gerhard or Gerhard Heinrich Geers at St. Nicolaus Catholic Church. His surname is often given as Gehrs. Gerhard was born about 1820 in Tütingen, Osnabruck, Niederscahen, Germany. Maria Catherine gave birth to their only child, Johann Heinrich Geers August 1, 1846. Sadly, Maria Catherine died five days later August

6, 1846 in Ankum from "kindbett" or childbirth complications. She was buried on August 8, 1846 in Ankum.

Her son, Johann Heinrich Geers, survived and eventually started another Gohmann family line of descendants. He married Anna Maria Starmann October 20, 1873 and immigrated to the United States, arriving August 5, 1890. He died February 2, 1926 in Hamilton County, Ohio. Presumably the widower Gerhard Heinrich Geers remarried. At some point, Gerhard Heinrich Geers also immigrated to the United States and died 1894 in Missouri. There is some evidence that he had, at least, a son with his second wife.

There is a strong possibility that the Geers were Colons; land owners. There are records of a Geers and Tüting marriage plus while emigrating, the Geers could afford to travel in ship's cabins rather than in steerage.

Death of Dirk Gohmann

The father of nine children, Johann Diedrich "Dirk" Gohmann, died January 18, 1841 in Ankum. The funeral Mass was offered at St. Nicolaus Catholic Church and he was buried in Ankum January 21, 1841. Dirk was 77 years old at the time of his death. Dirk Gohmann's widow, Maria Adelaid (Schulte) Gohmann, possibly then lived with one her adult children, likely Henry and his wife, Elisabeth, in Westerholte, near Ankum.

Gohman Timeline in Germany
(Gohman family present in Ankum from 1793 to 1846)

About 1729	Birth of Johann "Dirk" Gohmann in Paddenberge (now Badbergen) Possible father of "Dirk" Gohmann and grandfather of "Diedrich" Gohmann
About 1764	Birth of Johann "Dirk" Gohmann
Nov. 26, 1793	Marriage of Dirk Gohmann and Anna Catherine Konnermann
Nov. 12, 1794	Birth of Herman Heinrich Gohmann
Oct. 15, 1796	Birth of Gerhard Heinrich Gohmann
July 13, 1799	Birth of Maria Elisabeth Gohmann
Sept. 22, 1802	Birth of Maria Adelaid Gohmann
Aug. 3, 1803	Death of Herman Heinrich Gohmann
Oct. 22, 1803	Death of Anna Catherine (Konnermann) Gohmann

Jan. 16, 1804   Marriage of Dirk Gohmann and Maria Adelaid Schulte

June 15, 1804   Death of Maria Adelaid Gohmann

Sept. 23, 1804   Birth of Anna Maria Elisabeth Gohmann

June 6, 1808   Birth of Johann "Dirk" Gohmann

Mar. 11, 1809   Death of Death of Johann "Dirk" Gohmann at 80 years old

May 26, 1811   Birth of Johann Heinrich Gohmann

Feb. 24, 1814   Death of Johann "Dirk" Gohmann

May 11, 1814   Birth of Johann "Diedrich" Gohmann (patriarch)

Nov. 5, 1817   Birth of Maria Catherine Gohmann

Jan. 14, 1826   Marriage of Gerhard Heinrich Gohmann and Wilhelmina Rehe

Aug. 8, 1831   Birth of Maria Elisabeth Gohmann (daughter of Gerhard and Wilhelmina)

Aug. 20, 1834   Immigration of Gerhard Heinrich Gohmann and Wilhelmina (Rehe) Gohman and Maria Elisabeth (child), arriving in Baltimore, Maryland on Aug. 20, 1834

Jan. 18, 1841   Death of Johann "Dirk" Gohmann at 77 years old—father of the family.

Jan. 26, 1841   Marriage of Johann Heinrich Gohmann and Maria Elisabeth Barlage

Dec. 29, 1843   Immigration of Johann Diedrich Gohmann to the United States, arriving in New Orleans on December 29, 1843 and disembarking on Jan. 2, 1844.

_____1845   Immigration of Johann Heinrich Gohmann and Maria Elisabeth Barlage, along with widow, Maria Adelaid (Schulte) Gohmann

Oct. 26, 1845   Marriage of Maria Catherine Gohmann and Gerhard Heinrich Geers

___1845-1846   Immigration of Maria Elisabeth Gohmann and Anna Maria Elisabeth Gohmann to Cincinnati, OH, United States

Aug. 1, 1846   Birth of Johann Heinrich Geers, son of Maria Catherine and Gerhard Heinrich Geers

Aug. 6, 1846   Death of Maria Catherine (Gohmann) Geers

Börger Family in Germany

This chapter will focus on the Börger family in Germany before immigration to the United States. This Börger family is part of the Gohman story because Johann Diedrich Gohmann and Marie Elisabeth Börger married in Cincinnati, Hamilton County, Ohio and started a great Gohman family which now claims thousands of descendants.

The history of the Börger family in Germany has been traced back to 1675. From 1675 until 1845 the Börger family lived in one geographical location; the farming areas surrounding Damme, in the district of Vechta, which is in the state of Niedersachsen or Lower Saxony, in northwestern Germany.

The farming areas surrounding Damme and belonging to the parish of St. Victor in Damme include the following small communities; Borringhausen, Ihlendorf, Oldorf, Ossenbeck, Osterdamme, Osterfeine, Reselage, Rüschendorf and Sierhausen. Each of these areas were comprised of several independent farms. The names of some of the farms are: Flöttel, Gers or Geers, Grever, Höltermann, Sandermann, Schröder, and Wilke. The names of these farming areas and farms appear in the St. Victor Catholic Church baptism, marriage and death records of the Börger family.

Six generations of the Börger family had lived in the Damme area for 170 years and when a family lives in one location for such a long time, there are many potential benefits. There were many relatives nearby, more support for one another, more knowledge about work opportunities, more involvement in church, society and social groups, and more financial resources to borrow from for ongoing needs. When immigration to the United States was being planned, they had more support from relatives and friends than was normally found.

One other result of the Börgers living in one area for such a long time was family expansion with many family groups having similar names and ages living across the area; including both Colons, the land owners, and Heuerlinger, the serf class. It is often uncertain which family or individual is identified in local event records causing uncertain or conflicting evidence about events.

The immediate family of Elisabeth Börger lived in the Ihlendorf area, a few miles east of Damme. They were a Heuerling family just like the Gohman family in Ankum. Their church records included the words "Grever LZ" or "Grever Leibzucht" which meant this family lived in a "Leibzucht" or Heuerling house on the Grever farm. "Leibzucht" and "Heuerling" had somewhat similar meanings. Whoever lived in the "Leibzucht" had the right to live in that house on a farm and to manage a small garden for their own needs, but had to work for the Colon, or farm owner, whenever needed.

Elisabeth Börger's Ancestors

Elisabeth Börger's Great-great-great-great grandparents

Johan Börger married Hille Heye November 5, 1674 in Damme. They had two children, Joes Arendt and Herman. The second child, Herman Börger, was born April 12, 1677. He became the great-great-great grandfather of Elisabeth.

Elisabeth Börger's Great-great-great grandparents

Herman Börger married Anna Sierhaus October 24, 1700 at St. Victor Catholic Church in Damme. Anna Sierhaus was from the area that was known as Sierhausen and is a short distance southwest of Damme. They had four children; Johan Henrich. Anna Elisabeth, Johan Herman, and Gerhard Herman. The fourth child, Gerhard Herman Börger, was born June 16, 1709. He became the great-great grandfather of Elisabeth.

Elisabeth Börger's Great-great grandparents

Gerhard Herman Börger was married three times; Catharina Margaret Sierhaus, Anna Catharina Dürstock, and Catharina Alheid Otting. After his first wife died, he married Anna Catherine Dürstock April 29, 1732 at St. Victor Catholic Church. They had three children; Johan Henrich. Johan Herman, and Christopher Heinrich. Gerhard and Anna Catharina's third child, Christopher Heinrich Börger, was born June 6, 1737. He became the great grandfather of Elisabeth. The third marriage produced no children.

Elisabeth Börger's Great grandparents

Christopher Heinrich Börger married Anna Margaret Börger September 8, 1758 at St. Victor Catholic Church. They had six children; Gerhard Henrich, Herman Heinrich, Johan Gerhard, Margaret Alheid, Anna Catharina, and Margaret Angela. Their third child, Johan Gerhard Börger, was born August 8, 1762. He became the grandfather of Elisabeth.

Elisabeth Börger's Grandparents

Johan Gerhard Börger was married twice. His first wife died six days after giving birth to their first child, presumably from childbirth complications. That child was Catherina Maria Börger. Then Johan Gerhard married Catherine Maria Bertelt August 14, 1798 at St. Victor Catholic Church. They had two children; Johan Bernard and Johan Herman. The first child, Johan Bernard, was born July 1, 1799. He became the father of Elisabeth.

Elisabeth Börger's Parents

The parents of Marie Elisabeth Börger married Wednesday, October 5, 1825 at St. Victor's Catholic Church in Damme. The witnesses for the wedding were Johan Mescher and Frank Schütte.

Elisabeth's father, Johan Bernard Börger, was born July 1, 1799 in Osterdamme, a short distance east of Damme. He was baptized at St. Victor Catholic Church in Damme. His godparents were Johan Bernard Fischer, Johan Bernard Pohlschneider, and Maria Alheid Börger.

Elisabeth's mother, Maria Engel (a Germanic version of Angela) was born August 28, 1803. Her parents were Bernard Mescher and Anna Dorothea Böckermann. The godparents for her baptism at St. Victor Catholic Church were Maria Kophanke, Alheid Schröder and John Henrich Grever. The Grever family owned a farm in the area of Ihlendorf. As a baptism sponsor it can be assumed that the Grever family had some connection to the Mescher family. Later, when Maria Engel Mescher married Johan Bernard Börger, the couple were accepted as a Heuerling family on the Grever farm which gave them the right to live in a "Leibzucht" home on the Grever farm.

The couple went on to have four children, three girls and one boy. After 18 years of marriage, Elisabeth's mother died. A church record indicates she died December 31, 1843 on the "Wilke farm" or other Wilke property in Ihlendorf. The Wilke family was a substantial land owner in the Ihlendorf area and it is unknown why Maria was there when she died. Her son, Henrich, also died there earlier in 1838.

Usually a father, who lost his wife by death and had children to care for, married again. However there was no record in Damme of a second marriage for Elisabeth's father. With the possible exception of some emigration records, there were no later records in Damme that could be specifically attributed to this Börger family. Johan Bernard Börger and two, possibly three, of his daughters emigrated shortly after his wife's death.

Elisabeth Börger and Siblings

All the children of Johann and Maria Börger were born on the "Grever farm" in Ihlendorf near Damme and baptized at the St. Victor Catholic Church.

Original St. Victor Catholic Church baptism font
used by the Börger family

The first child was Maria Elisabeth Börger, born September 15, 1826. The godparents for her baptism were Maria Elisabeth Holthaus, Engel Holthaus and Joseph Luhrmann. When Maria Elisabeth was about 18 years old, she immigrated to the United States. When she was 19 years old, she married Johann Diedrich Gohmann in Cincinnati, Hamilton County, Ohio and they became parents and founders of the large Gohman family described in this book.

Excerpt of typed transcription of
Maria Elisabeth Börger's original baptism record

The second child was Maria Agnes Börger, born November 11, 1828. The godparents for her baptism at St. Victor Catholic Church were Maria Elisabeth Grever, Maria Alheid Schröder and Johan Henrich Wönker. As a teenager, Maria Agnes also immigrated to the United States.

The third child was Henrich Börger, born August 17, 1831. The godparents of his baptism were Henrich Böcker, Henrich Grever and Anna Maria Mescher. Henrich died at the age of 7 December 11, 1838 on the "Wilke farm" or other Wilke property in Ihlendorf. It is unknown why Henrich was there when he died.

The fourth child was Elisabeth Bernadine Börger, born July 21, 1834. The godparents of her baptism were Lisette (Meyer) Grever, Catharine Maria Böckermann and Johan Mescher. It is likely Elisabeth Bernadine would have immigrated to the United States to be with the rest of her family.

Decision, Planning, and Migration

When members of the Gohman and Börger families decided to emigrate from Germany and to immigrate to the United States, they were motivated by a dream. That dream made them daring enough to cross vast waters and ride the waves of unfathomable change. In making preparations for this trip they had to deal with many challenges.

Preparations for emigration

As Heuerlinger, the Gohman and Börger families belonged to the working poor with little opportunity to save for the basic expenses of transatlantic and cross country travel. Beginning in the mid 1700's, emigrants from Germany did not come to the Americas singularly or in families but rather in organized groups. They generally made the voyage and interior travel in groups from a village or area.

Ships were scheduled from Bremen, Germany to the United States according to the season. Typically a ship would only depart from Bremen to New Orleans in the spring and fall. New York and Baltimore had regularly scheduled trips but ships were no longer departing Bremen for Philadelphia.

Passage from Bremen, Germany to the United States varied according to the destination and age of the emigrant. If the average price of the total emigrants embarked did not meet what was required by the ship owners, each passenger price was adjusted upward. In 1835, one agent published passage prices to New Orleans, Louisiana, United States. His prices at the time were:

> *for each person over 12 years, 10 Pistolen, or 50 Reichsthaler, or 100 Rheingulden,*
> *for each child from 8 - 12 years 7½ Pistolen, or 37½ Reichsthaler, or 75 Rheingulden,*
> *for each child from 6 - 8 years 5 Pistolen, or 25 Reichsthaler, or 50 Rheingulden,*
> *for each child from 1- 4 years 2½ Pistolen, or 12½ Reichsthaler, or 25 Rheingulden,*
> *for each child up to 1 year 1 ¼ Pistolen, or 6 ¼ Reichsthaler, or 12 ½ Rheingulden,*

These prices were usually adjusted to achieve an average passenger price for the voyage of between 37 ½ to 40 Reichsthaler or 75 to 80 Rheingulden. The following mid-1800s European/German monetary information may give some idea of the value associated with cost of travel:

> Most German coins were linked to the Vereinsthaler, a silver coin containing 162 $^2/_3$ grams of pure silver. Later, the German mark was based on gold rather than silver and a fixed exchange rate between the Vereinsthaler and the mark of 3 marks = 1 Vereinsthaler was used for the conversion.

> Pistolen is the French name given to a Spanish gold coin in use in 1537. Later it was applied to other European gold coins of about the value of the Spanish coin. A coin with the same name was minted in Scotland with a weight of 106 grains of gold.

> Early Prussia adopted a Reichsthaler or thaler containing $^1/_{14}$ of a Cologne mark of silver. During the early 1800s a new Prussian standard for the Reichsthaler replaced the earlier standard. The thaler was worth 1¾ Gulden. It was also called Hannovarian Thaler, Hesse-Kassel Thaler, Mecklenburg Thaler and Saxon Thaler.

> The Rheingulden was minted by several German states encompassing the commercial centers of the Rhein (Rhine) River valley using a standard of 98% gold and 3.54 grams. By the time of the Holy Roman Empire the standard was 91.7% gold.

The earliest emigrants were often penniless and had to finance their passage. To do so, they agreed to become "indentured servants" also known as "redemptioners" or "servs". Typically, they signed a contract with a recruiter or ship's captain to repay the fare plus a stipend within a certain but short period. If they could not, they would enter a form of servitude, often including their family, for a given period, usually three to four years. Over half of all early German emigrants financed their passage in this manner. However, passage from Bremen normally required the emigrant to have some available money.

By the mid 1800's, two additional methods of financing the emigrant's passage became acceptable. Land grant companies and American employers sent out recruiters across rural Germany. If a German had saved a few dollars he was a target for land grant companies who paid a bounty to recruiters for each recruit that could possibly afford to buy land after arriving in America. Employer recruiters were looking for able bodied men who were offered jobs with a requirement to work at a minimal wage for a specific period. In return, they received passage to the employer's location. The recruiters traveled from village to village signing up groups of individuals and families desiring to emigrate. Often the recruiters used unethical "promises" to sign up a potential emigrant as they were paid a "bounty" or "bail" for as much as $70 for each recruit. It was a huge sum of money during that time.

New arrivals often initially settled in large cities and even chose indentured service to use the time to increase their starting capital. The dream of many German immigrants was to own a farm debt-free. Over and above the cost of their passage, they would have needed savings equivalent of at least $50 to $150 which was sufficient for a down payment on a farm large enough to support a family. They would also have needed an additional savings equivalent of $50 to $100 for farm startup and to carry them to the first harvest.

To pay for his passage and follow through on his dream, John Diedrich Gohmann most likely used a combination of accumulated savings and indentured service; a commitment to work for a Cincinnati employer.

The Gohman and Börger family members could never expect to return to their homeland in Germany. Emigration meant "letting go" of the past. It was both a great sacrifice and a liberation for the sake of their dream. Local government officials were even known to have told emigrants that they would not be welcomed back if their plans to live in the United States failed.

Sea Passage Fears

Typical Heuerling families, the Gohman and Börger families did not know the sea. With no seafaring experience, their dreams were mixed with fears. What they knew came from newspapers and stories passed from those that had experienced sea travel. They had heard that:

> For weeks immigrants lived on ship below tourist class in what was called steerage, often treated as immigrant freight along with other cargo loaded together on board in the lower deck.

> Usually each day immigrants got a bowl of soup. What money immigrants had was sewn into their clothes which they wore; pick-pockets were always around. Immigrants were only free to share their dreams and fears with a small group on board, with others from the same villages or farming areas or relatives.

> Sickness was always a threat on board; the immigrants facing the uncertainty of sickness preventing them from being accepted by the authorities and being rejected because of an illness and sent back home.

> Fear was always present of being lost at sea, the ship burning, and never being seen or heard from again.

The special immigrant joy of the first sight of land would have been mixed with fear of what would happen once they arrived. Immigrants landed on the shores of large metropolitan cities which was much different from their background of being farmers and country folk, increasing their fear. Uncertainty and few funds to deal with the unexpected also added to those fears.

Arrival in the United States

The travel time from Europe to the United States for an immigrant sailing ship in the mid-1840s ranged from six weeks to three months or even longer; depending on the ship, winds, tides and the sailing expertise of the captain and crew. During the 1850s, steamships became available for transatlantic travel and travel time became far less, two to five weeks. But for many decades the poorer class of immigrants continued to travel in sailing ships where the fare was cheaper and the passenger service continued to be barely tolerable.

If immigrants disembarked on the east coast of the United States, they would enter the country through New York City, Philadelphia or Baltimore. If they disembarked on the south coast of the United States, they would enter through New Orleans or Galveston. Immigrants wanting to get to Cincinnati from the east coast traveled by road and river until they got to the great Ohio River which would take them southwest to Cincinnati. Immigrants landing in New Orleans would have traveled north on the great Mississippi River until they reached the Ohio River and then traveled northeast to Cincinnati.

Ship records called Ship Manifests usually included the name of the ship, the captain's name, place and date of departure, place and date of arrival and a list of passengers and other cargo on board. Many passenger lists have survived in various archives, others are not yet published or have been destroyed. Individuals who died during ocean travel were buried at sea and often were not included on passenger lists made at the port of arrival.

Gohman Family Members who migrated

Five of the nine children of Dirk Gohmann immigrated to the United States along with, possibly, Dirk Gohmann's second wife, Maria Alelaid (Schulte) Gohmann. The other four children and their father, Dirk Gohmann, died and were buried in Ankum, Germany. The family did not all travel together but, rather, made the daring and demanding journey at different times and on various passenger ships.

Immigrant Gerhard Heinrich Gohman, wife and child

The first Gohman family member to immigrate was Gerhard Heinrich Gohman, the second child of Dirk Gohmann and Anna Catherine Konnermann. Gerhard Heinrich had married Wilhelmina Catherine Josepha Rehe from Bersenbrück January 14, 1826. They had one child while living in Germany; she was born August 8, 1831. Her name was Maria Elisabeth but was known as "Ana." After being married for eight years, the family decided to immigrate to the United States in 1834.

The family traveled on the Ship Cassander which left the port of Bremen, Germany and arrived at the port of Baltimore, Maryland August 20, 1834. The passengers were able to disembark two days later August 22nd. The Captain of the ship was W.D. Robinson. If Captain Robinson planned to take the shortest route, he would have traveled through the North Sea and the English Channel southwest across the Atlantic Ocean, a distance of 3800 nautical or 4373 statute miles. A notation in the Boston Post newspaper for August 28, 1834 stated that it took 60 days for Ship Cassander to travel from Bremen to Baltimore, which meant that the ship left Bremen about June 22, 1834.

The list of passengers numbered a total of 44 men, women and children. Some of these passengers remained connected to Gerhard and Wilhelmina in the years ahead. Some were from Ankum and Bersenbrück and other nearby towns and farming areas. They remained connected in their new homeland because they came from the same area in Germany, their immigration was organized by the same ship broker, and they became friends during their sea passage. After landing in Baltimore and completing the registration process, Gerhard and Wilhelmina followed the trail of immigrants to Cincinnati, Hamilton County, Ohio.

Five months before Gerhard Heinrich and Wilhelmina Gohman and their daughter, Ana, arrived in Baltimore, the State of Pennsylvania had completed the Main Line of Public Works, a system of early railroads, canals and inclined planes pulling wagons over the Allegheny Mountains. The new system connected Philadelphia to Pittsburgh where the Ohio River is created by the Allegheny River from the northeast and the Monongahela River from the south. Passengers could make this trip from the east coast to Pittsburgh in about five days at the cost of $10.00 per person, a vast improvement over earlier travel; walking, using horse-drawn carriages and ferry boats. It is not known whether this Gohman family was able to use this new system but, in any case, they arrived in Cincinnati, Hamilton County, Ohio and began their new life.

Immigrant Johann Diedrich Gohmann

The second Gohmann family member to immigrate to the United States was Johann Diedrich Gohmann. As the main character in this book, the story of his travel continues in later chapters.

Immigrant Johann Heinrich Gohman, wife and child and mother

The third Gohman family member to immigrate to the United States was Johann Heinrich Gohmann, known as John Henry Gohmann. He immigrated with his wife, Elisabeth (Barlage) Gohman, and, possibly, his widowed mother, Maria

Adelaid (Schulte) Gohman. According to an Ankum, Germany record, they emigrated in 1845 but according to Henry's Naturalization Intent documents, they arrived in New Orleans January 1, 1847. Some assume that they made an effort to be in Cincinnati for the wedding of John Henry's younger brother, Diedrich, on November 23, 1845. However, neither John Henry nor Elizabeth are listed as witnesses for that wedding.

No record has been found in Cincinnati confirming that the widowed mother arrived there safely. The rigors of traveling on the long voyage to the United States and then to Cincinnati may have been too strenuous for her and it is possible that she died along the way.

No record of the passenger ship has been found that brought John Henry, Elisabeth or Maria Adelaid to the United States.

Immigrants Maria Elisabeth and Anna Maria Elisabeth Gohman, sisters

It is very likely, two other Gohman family members immigrated to the United States. They are Maria Elisabeth Gohman and her half-sister, Anna Maria Elisabeth Gohman. However, no record was found in the Ankum archives that they married or died in Ankum. No record has been found of the passenger ship that brought them to the United States. It would have made sense for them to immigrate in 1845 along with John Henry and his wife Elisabeth and the widowed mother of Anna Maria Elisabeth, John Henry and John Diedrich. They also could have immigrated as two unmarried women traveling together on a separate ship. If they immigrated in 1845, Maria Elisabeth would have been 45 years old and Anna Maria Elisabeth would have been 41 years old. It is possible that on April 5, 1847 either Maria Elisabeth or Anna Maria Elisabeth served as the godmother for the baptism of John Bernard "Barney" Gohman, the first child of Diedrich and Elisabeth (Börger) Gohman at St. John the Baptist Catholic Church in Cincinnati.

Immigrant Johann Heinrich Geers and family

Another direct line descendant of Dirk Gohmann immigrated to the United States. Johann Heinrich Geers, the son of Gerhard Heinrich and Maria Catharine (Gohman) Geers, and the grandchild of Dirk Gohmann, survived into adulthood, married, had a family of four children and immigrated to the United States. Johann Heinrich married Anna Maria Elizabeth Starmann October 20, 1873 in Bersenbrück, near Ankum. She was born July 30, 1852 in Germany and later died there. Johann and Anna's first child was Catherine C. Geers, born May 18, 1876 in Germany. Their second child was Elisabeth B. Geers, born about 1884 in

Heeke, Osnabrück, Niedersachsen, Germany. Their third child was Anna Maria Geers, born March 16, 1885 also in Heeke. Their fourth child was Henry Antony "Harry" Geers, born February 25, 1890 in Germany. Johann Heinrich Geers and his four children immigrated to the United States in 1890.

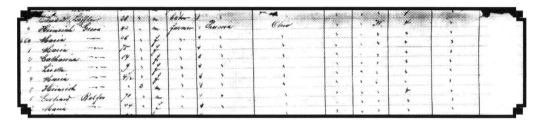

Excerpt of the Ship Karlsruhe passenger manifest

They sailed on the Ship Karlsruhe from Bremen, Germany and arrived in Baltimore, Maryland, United States on August 5, 1890. The Geers family traveled as cabin passengers which is a significant upgrade from steerage, the lowest class on board. The family spent some time in the State of Delaware before migrating to Cincinnati, Ohio.

Börger Family Members who migrated

The emigration story of the Börger family is not well documented and quite confusing. With the Börger family living in the Village of Damme and surrounding area for many generations, a great many related Börgers lived there. Many carrying on a Börger given name tradition resulting in many individuals with the same given name. From July 1834 to March 1849, three Börger families and six Börger individuals are known to have emigrated from Damme, Germany. During the years before and following, a large number of other Börgers also emigrated. Almost all had a destination of Cincinnati, Hamilton County, Ohio. The records of their movements were often uncertain and confusing. One of the situations encountered was that during the fifteen years important to this Börger story four men with variations of the given name of Heinrich emigrated. The family group of Elisabeth's father's first cousin, Johan Heinrich Börger, is listed in two very different ways. Their emigration document lists them as *"Heirich Boerger -3/1849 - Damme Village - farmer, with w___(?) & 1 c over 15 yrs, destination Cincinnati"*. That is a farmer with his wife and child over fifteen years old. Their immigration documents state they arrived May 1, 1849 and list them as:

123 Heinrich Borgen	*53 Damme*	*farmer*	*Oldenburg*
124 Marie Engel Borgen	*50 Damme*		*Oldenburg*
125 Marie Agnes Borgen	*20 Damme*		*Oldenburg*

No emigration or immigration records have ever been found that could be confirmed as being for John Bernard Börger or his daughters; Maria Elisabeth, Maria Agnes or Elisabeth Bernadine. It was also found that John Bernard was a common given name among the Börgers. Documents containing that name may or may not refer to Elisabeth's father. The same can be said for his daughters, Maria Elisabeth and Maria Agnes.

There is a very slim possibility that Elisabeth's father, John Bernard Börger, immigrated to the United States in the late 1830s and settled in Minster, Auglaize County, Ohio. It is 106 miles north of Cincinnati. Someone by that name died there in 1840. Minster was a German settlement starting in the early 1830s and named for Mŭnster, Germany. If accurate, John Bernard immigrated ahead of his family to prepare a place for his wife and his three daughters. The premature death of that John Bernard might have been caused by one of the cholera epidemics that swept through the Ohio immigrant communities.

There is a better possibility that John Bernard Börger and his daughters emigrated during 1844. If Diedrich Gohmann and Elisabeth Börger did not know each other until they met in Cincinnati, 1844 makes sense. This assumption would allow for a courtship period after Diedrich and Elisabeth met in Cincinnati and decided to marry on November 23, 1845.

Another good possibility is that the Börgers emigrated January 1845. It is known that a John Bernard Börger emigrated from Damme during that month. An Elisabeth Börger also emigrated that same month but was listed separately. It is not known if they traveled together or separately. No immigration records specifically attributed to them have been found. They would have arrived in Cincinnati in plenty of time for the upcoming wedding.

It is also known that other related Börger family members immigrated to the United States, went to Cincinnati, and then also moved to Minnesota. Some of these Börgers had the same names as the family of Elisabeth and the relationships are not all fully understood.

This much is known for certain, at some point, Marie Elisabeth Börger immigrated to the United States and settled in Cincinnati, Hamilton County, Ohio. There, she married Diedrich Gohmann on November 23, 1845. A number of Börgers were in the area and some were in attendance at the marriage.

Sea Passage on the Ship Agnes

There are two stories passed down within the Gohman family about how their ancestor, Diedrich Gohmann, traveled from Germany to the United States. Both stories were passed down from generation to generation and also preserved in a semi-official format; notations in the family bible and in a grandchild's recollection that was published in the Minnesota Historical Society files.

The first family story was written in German script and preserved in a family bible. The translation of this story stated:

> *"In 1844 my Great Grandfather, John D. Gohmann and a friend came to America from Hanover, Germany. They sailed across the ocean on a clipper ship. Landing in New Orleans he made his way to Cincinnati, Ohio."*

Another similar version supported New Orleans as the port of arrival:

> *"He (Diedrich Gohmann) immigrated to the United States between 1835 and 1844. He and a friend came over on a small sailboat. After landing at New Orleans, they made their way up the Mississippi and Ohio Rivers to Cincinnati, Ohio."*

The other family story as published in the Minnesota Historical Society Files, stated that Diedrich landed on the east coast of the United States:

> *"On May 23, 1812 our grandfather, John Dederick Gohman, was born in Hannover, Germany. Grandfather and another man came to America in 1835 or 1844. They came over on a small sail boat and landed on the east coast of America. Then they made their way through forests and wilderness to Cincinnati, Ohio."*

It is clear from a record found in Ankum, Germany that Diedrich Gohmann left there and immigrated to the United States in 1843. This record included a list of emigrants who left Ankum and the surrounding area. It is called "Auswanderer Ankum—Nordamerika—von 1834—1855." This list of immigrants was assembled from local official records by Margaret van der Haar of

Ankum. The list includes, under the year 1843, a Gohman "emigrtade" from Tütingen, that is, from the farming area south of Ankum where the Gohman family were Heuerlinger. This person was a "Dienstknecht," that is, a male servant. He was traveling alone since no other family member were listed with him. And he had 25 Thalers (one of the types of coinage in use at that time) in his possession. He had this much cash left over after paying for personal needs for the trip, paying for some of the traveling fees not covered by a bondage agreement with a travel agent or head hunter, and what he was willing to declare. He likely had other money hidden away in his personal belongings.

| 1843 | Gohmann | | Dienstknecht | Tütingen | 1 | 25 |
| 1845 | Gohmann | | Wwe. | Westerholte | 3 | 80 |

Excerpt from the "Auswanderer Ankum—Nordamerika—von 1834—1855"

An index of Diedrich's Naturalization Declaration of Intent indicated that Diedrich Gomann, age 35, from Hanover, departed from the port of Bremen on September 7, 1843 and arrived at the port of New Orleans on January 2, 1844. The surname "Gomann" was one spelling of the Gohman name during Diedrich's years in Cincinnati. It was possible that Diedrich never learned how to read or write. If so, the spelling of his name might not have been an issue for him. The age of 35 years listed on this Index supposedly was Diedrich's age at the time he made his Declaration of Intent. Actually he was three years older at that time. The actual Naturalization Declaration of Intent document was later found and gave somewhat differing information including a departure date of September 27, 1843 and an arrival date of January 2, 1844.

The search for the passenger ship that brought Diedrich to the United States required finding a ship that left Bremen September, 1843 and arrived in New Orleans late December, 1843 or early January, 1844 and had a passenger with a name close to Diedrich Gohmann. Eventually the Ship Agnes was discovered.

On October 10, 1843, Diedrich Gohmann joined the crew and other passengers on board the Ship Agnes in Bremen Harbor. The passenger manifest listed 224 passengers including a Catherine Gohmann. So many of the remaining passengers came from Ankum, Germany, and the surrounding area that it appears this group of immigrants was formally organized. Amongst the passengers on the manifest were names that would become familiar as Gohman neighbors in Cincinnati, Hamilton County, Ohio and eventually St. Augusta, Stearns County, Minnesota.

Excerpt of the Ship Agnes passenger manifest

Situated near the coast of Northern Germany, Bremen and its adjacent harbor were located on the river Weser about 37 miles south of where the river opens into the North Sea. The harbor, formerly known as the North Sea Harbor of Vegesack became part of Bremen 40 years earlier in 1803. The original harbor within the city of Bremen was accessible to the sea via the River Weser. It became nearly impossible to navigate to the original harbor because of severe river silting. Bremen was forced to acquire Vegesack as its new harbor. The combined city and port also became known as Bremerhaven. In the mid 1800's, Bremen or Bremerhaven was a major ship building center, an important cargo transshipment point, and was becoming a major point of departure for immigration to Canada, Australia, and the United States. Many sailing and even early steam vessels were being built in Bremen solely for the emigration business.

In 1832, the port of Bremen was the first municipality of any kind to initiate a law for the purpose of protecting emigrating Europeans. It was called the "Ordiance über die Auswanderung auf in-order ausländischen Schiffen Reisen" The English translation is the "Ordinance Concerning the Emigration Traveling on Domestic or Foreign Ships". In addition to other protections, it created the first requirement that ship owners must maintain passenger lists.

In 1851 the Bremen Chamber of Commerce established the "Nachweisungsbureau für Auswanderer" or the "Information Office for Emigrants" where the ship captains had to deliver their passenger lists. The rules and regulations of the 'Nachweisungsbureau' considerably improved the quality of both the emigrants stay at Bremen prior to taking passage and, somewhat ensured, the seaworthiness of the ships engaged in the emigration trade.

Unfortunately, sometime after 1911 and before 1920, all passenger lists from 1875 – 1908, older than 3 years, were destroyed due to lack of space in the Bremen Archives. With the exception of passenger lists for the years 1920 - 1939 all other lists were lost in World War II. The saved lists had been hidden in a salt mine and at the end of WWII were transferred into the custody of the "Allies". Between 1987 and 1990 those lists were once more back in the archives of the Bremen Chamber of Commerce. An agreement in July 1999, led to the digitizing of the passenger lists and their public availability.

Importantly for genealogists, many of the "Ordiance" regulations became the basis of regulations in other ports around the world and the requirement for ocean shipping passenger lists became universal.

Historically and even to this day, the name Agnes was and is a popular name for ships of all kinds. In 1843 there were many ships carrying the name Agnes; sailing vessels large and small, steam ships, paddle wheelers, and even a racing schooner yacht. The Ship Agnes that Diedrich Gohmann boarded on that eventful day in October had been built in Bremen especially for the emigration trade. It had been launched shortly before March 11, 1842 when it made its first voyage to New Orleans. A second sailing vessel named Agnes but rigged as a schooner was launched in Bremen in May and should not be confused with this passenger ship.

It is known that Ship Agnes made as many as two round trips to the American ports each year and was a regular visitor to New Orleans. During one of those visits a log of the visit was made by a New Orleans official which included the following description. Ship Agnes was described as displacing 590 tons with an 18 foot draft while loaded and carried 225 passengers on that trip. From this description and the use of the term "Ship" in association with her name, it was clear that she was a fully rigged sailing vessel of average size for that class. Ship Agnes carried a brigantine rig of at least three masts, those masts being square rigged. She was known both as Ship Agnes and Ship Schonerbrigg or Brigantine Agnes. For the rest of this chapter Ship Agnes will be called Agnes. It is known that sailing vessels during that time period often had their rigging changed to reflect the passage and cargo that was to be carried on any given trip. Because Agnes made routine immigration trips to America, it is safe to say that she was a fully rigged ship for the Diedrich Gohmann passage to New Orleans.

In addition to the three masts, Agnes most likely had two decks, possibly a decorative figurehead on its bow and either a flat or rounded stern. A description of a sister ship, Ship Meta, which had a similar displacement and was completed in Bremen in 1842, indicates that Agnes most likely was about 116 feet long and had a beam of about 27 feet. The upper deck had as many as 10 cabins and the lower deck could accommodate as many as 200 plus steerage passengers. The ship's speed was determined by the direction and speed of the prevailing winds.

Picture is of a similarly rigged sailing ship

The Master or Captain of Agnes was H. Bosse, sometimes incorrectly translated from German script as Basse, who was an experienced ship's master. He had made an earlier passage to New Orleans plus two passages to Baltimore. He had commanded the Ship Friedrich Jacob in 1839 on a passage to Baltimore before assuming the command of Agnes for an 1842 passage to New

Orleans. He continued to command Agnes until January 1, 1847 when he took command of the Ship Itzstein & Welcher. During his entire career, Master Bosse routinely took his ships to New Orleans, occasionally to Baltimore, and once to New York. Master H. Warnken became the master of Agnes after H. Bosse. Later in 1847, under the new master, the Agnes became infamous as the "ship of horrors" during a disastrous trip between Bremen and New York that actually ended up in Quebec, Canada.

The October 10th departure date was well chosen. Agnes would transit the North Sea and North Atlantic before extreme winter weather would set in. The ship would also transit the more southern waters and the Gulf of Mexico after the worst of the hurricane season was over. Despite the fortunate timing of the passage, life on board ship as a steerage passenger was anything but comfortable. Depending on the direction and speed of the prevailing winds, the passage times from Bremen to New Orleans varied significantly. The documented transit times for Agnes vary from a short 52 days to a longer and more common 73 days. The passage that Diedrich Gohmann experienced was even longer, 80 days.

At 590 tons, Agnes provided some small private cabins for those few immigrants who could afford that level of privacy and comfort. The majority of the immigrants, including Diedrich Gohmann, traveled in steerage in unimaginable conditions. The passengers were allowed to bring with them a small amount of personal property which went into the hold of the ship. In addition, they hand carried sufficient clothing, eating utensils, and other necessities to last for the expected duration of the voyage.

Because of weather and ship operation activity on the top deck, little opportunity existed for the steerage passengers to come "topside" and get fresh air. Below on the steerage deck, the passengers found dark, congested, and stifling conditions. Likely, there were two temporary partitions, one forward and one aft. The center section was for families and the other two for single men and women, respectively. Typically there was a long narrow bench down the center of the steerage deck. It was used for seating, eating, and other necessary tasks. On either side of the bench were rows of wooden bunks, stacked two high with storage under the bottom one. The ship's hatches were the primary source of light and ventilation. The hatches could only be opened in the best of weather and in fairly calm sea conditions. The remainder of the time, the hatches remained closed. When allowed, oil lamps provided the only other light. While providing that limited light, the oil lamps were very dangerous and also contributed to the poor air quality on the steerage deck.

After about a week at sea, the quality of the food and its preparation began to deteriorate. Meals generally consisted of preserved, salted meat, a bread or cracker of sorts, a grain mush or oatmeal, and dried beans or peas. The meals were prepared in a common galley and then brought down to the steerage deck to eat. Drinking water was no longer fresh and was in limited quantities. Buckets of salt water were used for washing and the lack of quality toilet facilities contributed to the passenger discomfort.

Contagious diseases were greatly feared during the mid-1800s and were an even greater risk on board the emigrant ships. The crowded conditions, seasickness, lack of sanitary conditions, tainted water, and ill-prepared food all contributed to that risk. Many people died in route. On this particular ocean transit and according to the ship's manifest, Agnes' crew and passengers escaped the loss of life that was so common on these voyages.

On December 29, 1843, Agnes arrived in New Orleans with Diedrich Gohmann and the other immigrants. Normally passengers were held on board the ship until all processing was completed. On January 2, 1844 Diedrich was allowed to disembark and begin his new life as an immigrant in the United States of America.

Diedrich found himself in a large city. During the previous decade, New Orleans had become the wealthiest and the third-most populous city in the United States. New Orleans was emerging as a major port with a booming cotton export business and ships arriving with immigrants from Ireland, France, and Germany.

Reconstructed
St. Louis Cathedral in New Orleans

Like others who were passing through, Diedrich would have made an early visit to St. Louis Square and St. Louis Cathedral. Unknown to Diedrich, but while he was there, the Baroness Pontalba was proposing to the Council for the First Municipality a project to create two-story arcaded facades to the front of buildings bordering St. Louis Square which she had inherited from her father. Eventually the project would give the Square a feeling of Paris, France that exists to this day. This project increased the need to reconstruct St. Louis Cathedral to bring its appearance to scale. As early as 1834, a need to increase the size of the Cathedral was recognized. The initial attempts to rebuild the Cathedral were a disaster but it was eventually completed.

Diedrich was fortunate to have arrived during the winter months. Immigrants who arrived in the spring or summer often were challenged by the "fevers" and other contagious diseases rampant during the heat of New Orleans' summers. Although much of the New Orleans population was French speaking, a large number of Germans had settled there after 1820. With many Germans in the community, Diedrich found some comfort in speaking his own language with them in this new land and sharing stories about their German homeland and the long passage across the ocean. Also these former countrymen offered some assistance in making plans for Diedrich's next journey northward on the Mississippi River to Cincinnati, Hamilton County, Ohio.

River Passage from New Orleans to Cincinnati

New Orleans was a good place for Diedrich to rest, reflect and imagine what lay ahead for him. He could sit along the harbor, walk under the recently installed oil street lamps and check out the new streetcar system. Most likely Diedrich spent only a few weeks in this beautiful and busy city. After he got back his "land legs," he was eager to move on. He knew that he could not settle down here. His spirit needed to remain strong and determined until he arrived where life for him could start anew.

In planning his trip to Cincinnati, Diedrich would have learned that the winter weather of 1843-44 was unusually mild and that the rivers further north would not be frozen over. There were three readily available means of transportation between New Orleans and Cincinnati. They were keel boats, packet boats, and scheduled long distance passenger boats. A keelboat was a low cost cargo boat and would have taken as much as six months to get to Cincinnati and arrival could be very uncertain. The packet boats generally carried mail over short scheduled routes and many transfers between boats would have been necessary.

The most realistic alternative available to Diedrich was the scheduled long distance passenger boat. These were quite fast for the day and served also as packet boats because they carried mail in addition to passengers. Two boats of this type were in regular Cincinnati service at the time, making round trips in about seventeen days. The total mileage on the rivers from New Orleans to Cincinnati, Ohio was about 1500 miles, including 1000 miles to Cairo, Illinois and then 500 miles to Cincinnati. Assuming that upriver was one day slower than the downriver trip, the round trip would have meant 9 days northward (or about 165 miles per day) and 8 days southward (or about 190 miles per day).

A local newspaper, The New Orleans Bee, published all the river steamboat arrivals and departures. From that information, Diedrich would have decided to travel on the Champion, departing

January 18, 1844 or February 5, 1844 or the Queen of the West, departing either January 19, 1844 or February 9, 1844. Information about later steamboats using the same names is available but no information can be found for these two earlier boats.

An individual steamboat paddle wheeler would be used for only four or five years. In that time frame, they were abandoned due to lack of maintenance, sunk due to river "snags," or their boilers blew up.

A description of a typical steamboat paddle wheeler for that time and place would be a side wheel, wooden hull packet, 266' x 34' x 8', 709 tons, multiple boilers, and 30' diameter paddlewheels. They had two decks, the boiler deck and the hurricane deck. He boiler deck was also called the main deck and was the location of most passenger accommodations such as cabins and saloons. The hurricane deck was above the boiler deck, usually the uppermost full deck on the boat. It was the deck with a view and usually with more comfortable breezy winds. Later in 1844, new boats had a third deck, the Texas deck which was a smaller deck on the top of the hurricane deck. It usually included the pilot house and a swank large passenger lounge. The Texas deck was named after the largest and newest State of the Union.

Steamboat paddle wheeler passenger manifests were very informal documents and are rarely found. Actual documentation of Diedrich's trip to Cincinnati is not available but timing and circumstances provide insight into his trip.

The published departure time for the four likely departure dates of the steamship Champion and the steamship Queen of the West was 4:00 PM. Diedrich would have observed the hustle and bustle of the boat's crew loading the cargo and mail. Passengers would be rushing to board before the departure time. Most impressive would be the sight of the smoke from the exhaust stacks of the steamboat boilers as the boat's engineer added fuel to build up steam. If he had left just one month later, he would have seen the steamboat, Pilot, explode with a great loss of life as it prepared for departure.

As Diedrich's steamboat paddle wheeler left New Orleans and proceeded up the Mississippi, he experienced very mild weather. The thermometer hit 70 in January and February for the areas around the lower Mississippi and Ohio rivers. The 1844 era steamboats carried only about twelve hours of wood to stoke the boilers which would have required about sixteen refueling stops. Some of the stops would be at towns and cities along the way and others would be at remote refueling yards that were established along the river. Most refueling stops were at the confluence of another river with the Mississippi. The refueling stops would provide Diedrich ample opportunity to see the local rural countryside and the towns along the river.

The first possible refueling stop at a town would have been Baton Rouge, Louisiana. Destined to become the state capital in a couple of years, at that time it was a small town with a population of about 5,000. Its commerce was centered on the river. The next possible stop at a town was

Natchez, Mississippi. This town was on a bluff overlooking the Mississippi River. Although a very small town, it had become a center of trade and was the entry point for the Natchez Trace, a historical path that extends all the way to Nashville, Tennessee. It served as an overland link to the Mississippi, Cumberland, and Tennessee rivers. As Diedrich was passing through, the town was becoming the home of many extremely wealthy Southern plantation owners. Each owned large plantations, growing cotton and sugar cane and shipping the crops on the Mississippi River.

Grand Gulf, Mississippi would have been the next likely refueling port. It was destined to become a ghost town and serve as a state military park. At the time it was a thriving small town that served the steamboats on the Mississippi River. Next was Vicksburg, Mississippi which would soon play a major part in the Civil War. In 1844 as Diedrich traveled north it was another key refueling station. Near Vicksburg was an alternative refueling point, Greenville, Mississippi. It was a small village that had been moved from its earlier location. During the Civil War battle for Vicksburg, Greenville was again destroyed.

Further up the river was another refueling point called Napoleon, Arkansas. It supported commerce on the Arkansas and Mississippi rivers and became famous in Mark Twain's book "Life on the Mississippi." It has since become a ghost town. Another small town refueling point, further north on the Mississippi River, was Helena, Arkansas.

The next refueling stop was the great city of Memphis, Tennessee, adjacent to Chickasaw Bluffs overlooking the Mississippi River. It was a major commerce stop and refueling point for the Mississippi steamboats. The city was the center of processing, marketing, and transporting cotton and was known as "King Cotton." Most likely Diedrich had his first real introduction to slavery in the American south during his stopover in Memphis. In 1844, the city's population was one fourth slaves.

The 1844 Memphis riverfront

As his steamboat traveled on, Diedrich likely arrived at New Madrid, Missouri, the last possible refueling stop on the Mississippi River. This town was known for a number of major earthquakes in the years before Diedrich made his trip.

Diedrich was fortunate to have been traveling during January or February of 1844 and not later during the spring and summer. The area around the confluence of the Missouri and Mississippi rivers received a huge amount of rainfall during late April and through May. The result was a June flood coming from the confluence of these two rivers down to and including the confluence of the Mississippi and Ohio rivers. It was known as the "Flood of 1844" and was considered one of the largest floods of all times. Diedrich avoided this flood by three or four months.

Cairo, Illinois is where the Mississippi and Ohio rivers meet. It was a boom town in the 1840s. Its founders planned on it becoming one of the country's greatest cities. When Diedrich was passing through, there was talk that the city would be bigger and grander than St. Louis, Louisville, and Cincinnati. There was even some talk of the city becoming the capitol of the United States. If Diedrich had been traveling eight months later, he might have heard some of the stories floating up and down the Ohio River about one of the deadliest steamboat explosions in history, the end of the Lucy Walker. It happened just out of the port of New Albany, Indiana about a two-day journey from Cairo, Illinois.

Most likely Paducah, Kentucky was the first stop on the Ohio River for Diedrich. It was the hub for steamboats as they traversed several smaller rivers. Beyond Paducah the next possible refueling stop was Evansville, Indiana. Then there was the major river port city of Louisville, Kentucky. Here the Falls of the Ohio were located near the city, a stretch of the river which dropped 26 feet in 2 ½ miles created by rock outcroppings and boulders in the river. It was a major issue for earlier steamboat travel until a local businessman in 1830 created the Louisville and Portland Canal. As a result Diedrich's steamship was able to bypass the falls in a matter of hours, another new experience for Diedrich.

Two more refueling points possibly delayed Diedrich's trip at Jeffersonville, Indiana and Vevay, Indiana. Finally, after a rather speedy river journey of about eight or nine days, Diedrich arrived in Cincinnati, Hamilton County, Ohio. Germans were among the earliest settlers of Cincinnati. Some of these German folk would have been on hand to welcome Diedrich and others from Germany.

After much planning, the long sea voyage, and the quick trip up the Mississippi and Ohio rivers, Diedrich finally could feel some rest in his tired bones and some welcome in his new home. He was ready to begin to live his dream.

Life in Cincinnati

Depending on his New Orleans departure date, Diedrich Gohmann arrived in Cincinnati, Hamilton County, Ohio either January 27, 1844 or February 18, 1844. Cincinnati was to be his home for the next twelve years.

Cincinnati was founded in 1788 at the spot on the north bank of the Ohio River directly opposite the confluence of the Licking River. Originally named "Losantiville" which is French for "The town opposite the mouth of the Licking River". In 1790, the name of the settlement was changed to "Cincinnati" in honor of an early military group called the Society of the Cincinnati. Cincinnati was incorporated as a city in 1819. The development of steam boats on the Ohio River in 1811 along with the completion of the Miami and Erie Canal helped forge Cincinnati into a booming city. The arrival of railroads shortly after 1836 further expanded the City's industrial and trading might and it became known as "Porkopolis" because of the size of its pork packaging industry. By the time, Diedrich arrived, Cincinnati had become the largest city in the United States and was known as the "Queen City". One historian estimated the three-fourths of the population was German and, at least, two-thirds were Catholic. Diedrich likely received a warm welcome from a supportive population.

Cincinnati waterfront circa 1844

To pay for his passage from Bremen, Germany to Cincinnati via New Orleans, Diedrich Gohmann most likely used a combination of accumulated savings and signing a contract to be indentured to work for a Cincinnati employer. From that, it is safe to assume that Diedrich reported immediately to the company or individual that he was indentured to. Housing and transportation, if necessary, would already have been arranged for him. Initially, he most likely lived in a boarding house on the north side of town, across the Miami Canal, in a neighborhood known as "Over-the-Rhine". Diedrich, initially, was a parishioner of the original, and now known as "Old" St. Mary's Catholic Church located at 123 East Thirteenth Street. While the lives of later Cincinnati Gohman's are well documented, little is known about the details of Diedrich's personal life in Cincinnati. However, a number of major events in Diedrich's life are documented and can be told here.

Likely still working in an indentured status, in 1845 Diedrich requested permission of his employer to marry. Normally, it was required by the indenture contract that a male employee remain a bachelor. In this case, an exception was made and Diedrich married Maria Elisabeth Börger November 23, 1845 at St. Mary's Catholic Church. The German community knew the church as "Marien-Kirch", the largest Catholic Church in the city. The priest who conducted the service was Fr. Joseph Fernending; he signed the Hamilton County marriage certificate as a "Minister of the Gospel". The marriage registry of the old St. Mary's Catholic Church indicates that Fr. Fernending performed two marriages that day. There were four witnesses to the marriage listed; John B. Wörnker, Agnes Börger, Hermann H. Hollenkamp and Elizabeth Brockamp.

Diedrich and Elisabeth Gohmann's marriage certificate

The union of Johann Diedrich Gohmann and Maria Elisabeth Börger made them the patriarch and matriarch of what would become a very large United Sates family. The next six years in Cincinnati went by quickly. Sometime before 1847, the couple became parishioners of the new St. John the Baptist Catholic Church which had been built earlier in 1845. It was located on the corner of Bremen and Greene streets. They had a son followed by two daughters; John Bernard "Barney" Gohman born Aril 4, 1847, Anna Marie Agnes Gohman born 1849, and Maria Elizabeth Gohman born September 8, 1851. The young family was struck by tragedy when Maria Elizabeth died just two days short of being one year old, September 6, 1852. The young couple also faced religious persecution during the early years of their marriage. Starting about 1848, a group called the "Freeman" were bringing anti-Catholic violence to the streets of Cincinnati. Catholics began organizing themselves into groups to resist the street violence.

During 1851 and 1852, Diedrich and his family were living just across the Miami Canal but out of the "Over-the-Rhine" district. They were living in a row house between Maple and Ash streets. Beginning in 1852, Diedrich often took his family to the Findlay Market. It was a nearby "Over-the-Rhine" marketplace that provided shopping and social gathering. All the "Over-the-Rhine" Germans could be found there on a regular basis and it became their community center.

A contemporary writer reported that the German women could keep up with the men as they lifted their "Bierseidels", German for beer steins, at the market.

By 1852, it is likely that Diedrich was free from his indenture contract and could begin planning and saving for the family's future. May 8, 1852 he applied for United States citizenship by appearing before J. M. McMasters, the Clerk of Court of Common Pleas in Hamilton County, Ohio and formally declaring his intent to become a citizen. Diedrich also moved his family back to the "Over-the-Rhine" district early in 1853. They then lived at 132 Liberty Street which was just around the corner from Diedrich's brother, Henry, who was living at 122 Pleasant Street.

At some point, a photographer named Lewis from Celina, Mercer County, Ohio set up a temporary studio in Cincinnati. Diedrich was one of his early customers.

Diedrich Gohmann's handsome portrait

Diedrich and Elisabeth welcomed into the world a new son, George Heinrich Gohmann, July 10, 1853. George Henry came into the world as Cincinnati continued to grow. About the time of his birth, Cincinnati hired its first police chief and began paying men to act as its fire department. It was the first full-time paid fire department in the United States and the first to use a steam fire engine. After a mandated two year waiting period, Diedrich made another appearance in the Hamilton County Court of Common Pleas. Diedrich became a citizen of the United States October 9, 1854.

The German Catholic immigrants were growing rapidly in numbers and were holding tight to their language and traditions. That growth led to settlement societies being formed in the early 1850s which encouraged resettlement to six Cincinnati daughter settlements including New Ulm in the Minnesota Territory. Future Gohman neighbors, Heinrich Anton Imholte and Johan Heinrich Fibbe joined one of the settlement societies and made an exploratory trip to the Minnesota Territory. With the encouragement of the Bishop, "German Catholic Churches" were multiplying across the city and German speaking schools were created.

Europe, especially Germany, was in political turmoil during the mid-1850s. Immigrants and others in the United States began taking up sides. When representatives of the Pope began to involve themselves in the European problems, the situation in Europe worsened and people in the United States began taking up sides. The Germans in Cincinnati actually formed several military groups to include an artillery battery! To add to the "bad blood" in Cincinnati, the German immigrants were resisting full integration into the population as a whole. The combination of events helped lead to a political party known as the "Know-Nothings" winning the April 2, 1855 Mayoral race in Cincinnati. Its platform was anti everything foreign especially foreign "papist Catholic" immigrants. The election appeared to validate the continuing ethnic and religious conflict. The days following the election were filled with rioting in the streets. The violence resulted in several German deaths. The disruption spread to other cities with large German populations. In Louisville, Kentucky the riots tuned into all out urban warfare.

Compounding the religious issues in Cincinnati, the German, Irish, and Dutch Catholics practiced their religion as isolated groups, often creating great friction between them. The increasing violence against the Catholic immigrants and the internal religious strive became over-riding reasons for many families to move on. Northern Ohio, the states of Kentucky and Wisconsin, and the Minnesota Territory became popular destinations. It was time for Diedrich and his family to move on!

In far-a-way South Carolina, a veteran of the "Florida War" also known as the 2nd Seminole War began transactions that would, in the near future, change the destiny of the Diedrich Gohmann family. During early 1855, Peter Hollis applied to the federal capital in Washington City, District of Columbia for a Bounty Land Warrant. He received the warrant, number 20.082 dated September 25, 1855 under "An act in addition to Certain Acts Granting Bounty Lands" for action in the Florida War also known as the 2nd Seminole War". The warrant gave Peter Hollis claiming rights, "locate on", to a plot of land in any federal land district. It is shown here.

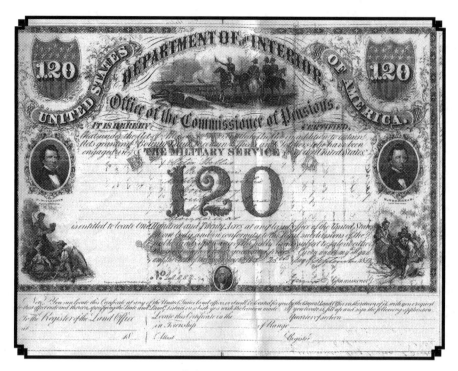

Peter Hollis' Bounty Land Warrant

After receiving the warrant and having no intention of relocating, Peter Hollis offered up his warrant for sale through land agents handling such warrants. This was common practice at the time and it just so happened that the agents were successfully selling warrants in Cincinnati. Most of the earlier warrants sold were used to claim land in an area known as the Virginia Military Territory. That land was generally to the south and east of Cincinnati. When new lands were made available in land districts further into the frontier, only the more adventurist dreamer considered them. Diedrich obviously met the description. Before long, Diedrich and a land agent concluded a deal for the sale of the Hollis warrant. After being informed of the transaction, Peter Hollis assigned his warrant to Diedrich. The record of the proceedings were dated February 9, 1856 and the action took place in the Court of Common Pleas, Military District of South Carolina.

Late February 1856, Diedrich got the word that the warrant had been reassigned and he could use it to claim 120 acres in any surveyed federal land district. One might guess that another son, John Diedrich Gohmann, is conceived as his future parents are celebrating.

Although Diedrich and Elisabeth had been planning and hoping for this turn of events, the next few weeks got hectic as they prepared to leave the home and security they had known in Cincinnati.

Other Gohmans in Cincinnati

A large population of German immigrants who used some variation of the Gohman name initially settled in the Cincinnati area. Some Gohmanns were known to have lived in Cincinnati prior to 1836. The other Gohmann immigrants included "wagon makers and painters", hostlers, shoe makers, drivers, sales ladies, and wood workers.

Joining the other German immigrants of Cincinnati were five of the nine children of Dirk Gohmann who had immigrated to the United States along with, possibly, Dirk Gohmann's second wife, Maria Alelaid (Schulte) Gohman. The family members did not all travel together but, rather, made their way separately to Cincinnati, Hamilton County, Ohio.

Immigrant Gerhard Heinrich Gohman, wife and child

Gerhard Heinrich Gohman with his wife, Wilhelmina Catherine Josepha (Rehe), and daughter, Maria Elisabeth (known as Anna) arrived at the port of Baltimore, Maryland August 20, 1834. After landing and completing the registration process, the family followed the trail of immigrants to Cincinnati, Hamilton County, Ohio. The couple then following other German families, moved on to Minster, Auglaize County, Ohio.

In 1837, a son, Gerhard Henry, was born to the couple. He was baptized April 6, 1837 at St. Augustine Catholic Church in Minster. The child died 1840.

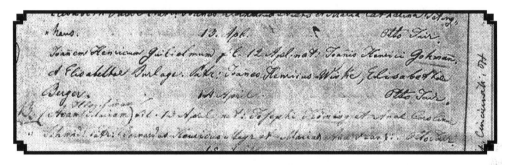

Gerhard Henry Gohman baptism record exerpt

A daughter, Catherina, was born in 1839. She was baptized January 5, 1839 and was also baptized at St. Augustine Catholic Church.

Gerhard died sometime between 1841 and 1842. Wilhelmine remarried to N.G. Norman July 25, 1842. N.G. Norman may have also been known as Heinrich Worman. If they are one and the same individuals, he was known to be a widower and his first wife was Maria Adelheid Dohmann.

Immigrant Iohann Heinrich Gohman, wife and child and mother

Johann Heinrich Gohmann, known as John Henry Gohman, immigrated with his wife, Elisabeth (Barlage) Gohman, and, possibly, his widowed mother, Maria Adelaid (Schulte) Gohmann. According to Henry's Naturalization Intent documents, they arrived in New Orleans January 1, 1847. No record has been found in Cincinnati confirming that the widowed mother arrived there.

Henry and Maria's first child, Diedrich Theodore, was born November 1848 and died January 11, 1849. Their next child, John Henry Gerhard, was born April 12, 1849 and baptized at St. John the Baptist Catholic Church in Cincinnati April 13, 1849.

September 11, 1850, the family was listed as living in Cincinnati's 10th Ward on the 1850 census. John Henry was listed as a laborer. In 1853, the city directory had him living at 122 Pleasant Street near his brother, Diedrich. In later city directories, John Henry was listed as a "varnish maker" and living at 94 Mohawk Street. The same directories list his son, John Henry Gerhard, starting out as a "wagon maker" and becoming a "car maker". He also lived at 94 Mohawk Street. Today, that address is a duplex and may have been one then. John Henry Gerhard was also sometimes known as William, went on to marry twice, and had four or five children. By 1857, John Henry was living at 522 Vine Street. His son, William eventually moved to 448 Race Street in 1864.

Henry appeared in the Hamilton County Court of Common Pleas April 18, 1853 and declared his intent to become a naturalized citizen.

Maria Elisabeth (Barlage) Gohman died April 29, 1874 in Cincinnati and was buried there in St. John the Baptist Cemetery. Johann died seven years later August 24, 1881 in Cincinnati and was also buried in St. John the Baptist Cemetery.

Immigrants Maria Elisabeth and Anna Maria Elisabeth Gohman, sisters

No record was found in the Ankum archives that Maria Elizabeth Gohmann and her half-sister, Anna Maria Elisabeth Gohmann, married or died in Ankum. It is very likely that the two women also were in Cincinnati. However, no record attributed to them has been found of the passenger ship that brought them to the United States. It would have made sense for them to immigrate in 1845 along with John Henry and his wife Elisabeth. They also could have immigrated as two unmarried women traveling together on a separate ship. If they immigrated in 1845, Maria Elisabeth would have been 45 years old and Anna Maria Elisabeth would have been 41 years old. It is possible that on April 5, 1847 either Maria Elisabeth or Anna Maria Elisabeth served as the godmother for the baptism of John Bernard "Barney" Gohman, the first child of Diedrich and Elisabeth (Börger) Gohmann at St. John the Baptist Catholic Church in Cincinnati. There are other Cincinnati records for individuals with similar names as the two sisters but they cannot be conclusively tied to them.

Immigrant Johann Heinrich Geers and family

After his wife died, Johann Heinrich Geers and children; Catherine C., Elisabeth B., Anna Maria, and Henry Antony "Harry" immigrated to the United States in 1890.

The family spent some time in the State of Delaware before migrating to Cincinnati, Ohio.

Other Börgers in Cincinnati

There were a large number of Börgers living in the Cincinnati, Hamilton County, Ohio during this time, many with similar names and birthdays. It is also known that other related Börger family members immigrated to the United States, went to Cincinnati, and then also moved to Minnesota. Some of these Börgers even had the same names and similar birthdates as the family of Elisabeth. Two Börger or Berger brothers, Henry and Gerhard, along with their mother Elisabeth "Lonnae" (Nüssen) Berger were also living in Cincinnati. Later in Minnesota, Henry would marry one of the Gohman offspring. The relationship of Elisabeth to all these Börgers/Bergers is not all fully understood.

Elisabeth's father, John Bernard Börger, could have immigrated during 1838, 1844 or 1845. The 1838 date is the least likely. However, he had arrived in time to serve as the godfather of John Bernard "Barney" Gohman, the first child of Diedrich and Elisabeth (Börger) Gohman, in Cincinnati, Hamilton County, Ohio on April 5, 1847. During 1849 and 1850, he lived with his daughter, Marie Agnes, on Abigail Street between Main and Sycamore streets. A widower, John Bernard Borger remarried to Mary Pillensoessel July 1, 1851.

Elisabeth's sister, Marie Agnes Börger is listed as a witness on the Diedrich and Elisabeth's marriage records. She also was a witness for their father's second marriage. Just over a year later, November 11, 1852, she died at age 23.

Elisabeth's sister, Elisabeth Bernadine Börger, may have also been in Cincinnati and possibly died there May 20, 1846. A St. Mary's burial record for a "Dina" Börger contains the correct age. There are several other records for Elisabeth Börgers but none that can be specifically attributed to Elisabeth Bernadine have been found in Cincinnati or elsewhere.

Elizabeth also had a second cousin named Maria Agnes Börger who was in Cincinnati at the time. She married Johan Heinrich Fibbe May 4, 1851. By 1857, that couple were also living near St Augusta, Stearns County, Minnesota. Many family members think that Elisabeth's sister and not her second cousin married Johan Fibbe. However the birthdate on Maria Agnes (Börger) Fibbe's tombstone is that of the second cousin's birthdate in church records in Damme, Germany. Also the cousin has much in common with the Fibbe family including traveling on the same ship when immigrating.

Only three things can be said for certain about the other Börgers in Cincinnati. A large number lived there. Many had come from the Damme area in Germany. And, a large number resettled in and around St. Augusta, Stearns County, Minnesota.

River Passage from Cincinnati to the Minnesota Territory

Preparations

Diedrich and Elisabeth Gohmann were not the only immigrant Germans who were positioning themselves for the next step in their dream of owning their own farm. Casper Klinkhammer, Henry Berger, and the Joseph Toenjes and Henry Witschen families were all doing the same thing. After acquiring land warrants, they were planning a departure to the Minnesota Territory as soon as the rivers were navigable in the spring of 1856. Notice of claimable land in the Sauk River Land District was being published in Cincinnati newspapers. Fr. Francis Xavier Pierz had articles published in the newspaper, Der Wahrheitsfreund (The Friend of Truth), encouraging German immigrants to come to the Minnesota Territory. He also had letters published in the Cincinnati Diocese "Catholic Telegraph" newspaper with the same encouragement. There is a strong possibility that Diedrich and others received a favorable report from future Gohman neighbors, Heinrich Anton Imholte and Johan Heinrich Fibbe who had joined a settlement society and made a scouting trip to the Minnesota Territory. Joining the other men and their families, Diedrich and family hurriedly put their affairs in order so as to make a departure on an unknown date.

The winter of 1855-1856 began unusually mild but then turned very cold and for a time froze over the Mississippi as far south as St. Louis, Missouri. Two December 12, 1855 announcements in the Dubuque, Dubuque County, Iowa, newspaper, Express and Herald stated:

> "The steamers Ben Coursin, Kate Cassel and Excelsior have laid up here for the season, as navigation is now considered closed."

> "The river is full of running ice and the sloughs are frozen over, so that the boys have commenced their winter sport of skating."

The ice got as thick as three feet in places during extreme cold weather in January which was followed by unseasonably warm weather in February. The sudden change in average temperature caused the ice to break into floes that came pushing down the river. In St. Louis, a great many river boats were tied up in rafts along the levees for the winter. It was said that the boats were tied up so close that one could walk from deck to deck for 20 city blocks. The huge ice floes collided with the rafts of river boats; tearing them loose, breaking them up and creating total destruction. The wreckage of the river boats combined with the ice floes lodged on an island just below St. Louis creating a dam. The Mississippi rose ten feet and began to refreeze in what became known as "The Great Mississippi Ice Gorge". When the gorge finally broke the ice flows and steamboat wreckage continued downstream causing more mayhem and destruction.

Mid-March 1856 the steamboat Lady Franklin was making preparations to leave Cincinnati for the city of St. Paul in the Minnesota Territory which was the northern most river steamboat terminal at the time. Departure would be as soon as river conditions permitted and fuel, supplies and cargo was being stowed. The Lady Franklin was owned by Galena, Dubuque, Dunleith, and Minnesota Packet Company. The large company was attempting to bring organized transportation to the upper Mississippi River. The master or captain of the river boat was M.E. Lucas. The Lady Franklin had been launched 1850 in Wheeling, West Virginia and was a side-wheel wooden hull packet with a displacement of 206 tons. Earlier in 1855, one voyage of the Lady Franklin brought 800 immigrants to St. Paul and a new life. It broke all records for number of passengers arriving there at one time. Especially noteworthy was the fact that the Lady Franklin's published capacity was only 500 passengers! The Lady Franklin was destroyed later in 1856 when it hit a snag October 23rd near the foot of Coon Slough Landing which was just below St. Paul. It sunk with the loss of five lives. The master, M.E. Lucas, was held responsible.

A picture of a sister ship of the Lady Franklin

Riverboat Adventure

Around March 24, 1856, Diedrich and his family joined Casper Klinkhammer, Henry Berger, and the Joseph Toenjes and Henry Witschen families in boarding the Lady Franklin. Shortly after the passengers were boarded and their personal effects stowed, the historic steamboat cast off on a voyage of a planned nine days to St Paul.

The Lady Franklin likely made two refueling stops out of five possible on the Ohio River before entering the Mississippi River. After two possible refueling points at Jeffersonville, Indiana and/or Vevay, Indiana, the Gohman family may have had time to debark while the steamboat refueled at the major river port city of Louisville, Kentucky. The family did experience by-passing the "Falls of the Ohio" through a series of locks in the Louisville and Portland Canal. Their steamboat was actually lowered 26 feet in 2 ½ miles.

Beyond Louisville, the next possible refueling stop was Evansville, Indiana and then Paducah, Kentucky. As during his first visit, Diedrich would have found Paducah to be a hub for steamboats as they traversed several smaller rivers.

Another place the Gohman family likely visited was Cairo, Illinois. It is located near the confluence of Mississippi and Ohio rivers. It was a boom town when Diedrich first visited it on the way to Cincinnati and its residents thought it would become the one of the country's greatest cities. During this visit, the town's plans were a bit less grandiose.

Shortly after entering the Mississippi, the Lady Franklin likely refueled plus unloaded and loaded cargo on the levees of St. Louis, Missouri. Recently damaged February 28, 1856 by the "The Great Mississippi Ice Gorge", the levees were still quite a sight for the travelers. The levees were originally surveyed and construction began by Lieutenant Robert E. Lee. Lieutenant Lee went on to become a General and known for his exploits during the United States Civil War. St. Louis was a rapidly growing center of commerce; fighting pollution, developing public schools, and becoming politically active.

The next likely refueling stop was the boyhood home of Mark Twain, Hannibal, Marion County, Missouri. He was 21 years old at the time and just beginning the adventures and writing that he was to become famous for.

The next stretch of the Mississippi River offered the master of the Lady Franklin choices between pairs of towns and cities on either side of the river to replenish supplies and fuel.

Davenport, Scott County, Iowa and Rock Island, Rock Island County, Illinois were the first pair. Rock Island Railroad built the first railroad bridge across the Mississippi River; finishing just before the Gohman family passed through in 1856. It connected Davenport to Rock Island. This railway connection would improve both transportation and commerce with Chicago. The new railway was a competitive threat to the river steamboats and May 6, 1856 a steamboat captain deliberately crashed his boat into the bridge. Benedictine priests traveling to St. Paul, Minnesota Territory described the incident somewhat differently.

> *"About 3 o'clock p.m., we left Davenport and had to pass beneath the C.R.I. railroad bridge, which crossed the river at this point at an oblique angle, a serious obstacle to navigation, especially during the spring floods. Our steamer struggled for nearly an hour trying to effect passage between the piers of the bridge. Fat and pitch were thrown into the furnace to raise steam-pressure to the utmost. We passed safely. Not so the steamer which ran in our wake. Its boiler exploded and its passengers were hurled to destruction. Two other steamers came up to offer assistance; they also burned and hundreds of lives were lost."*

Later, the owner of the steamboat filed a lawsuit against the railroad company. Abraham Lincoln was the lead defense lawyer for the railroad company and successfully defended it all the way to the United States Supreme Court.

The next pair of towns; Dubuque, Dubuque County, Iowa and Galena, Jo Daviess County, Illinois, would both have been good choices for the next refueling stop. Both were rapidly becoming major centers of operation for steamboats plying the waters of the upper Mississippi River. Since Galena was a homeport of the owners of the Lady Franklin, there is no doubt that the Gohman family visited there. They saw many steamboats and other river boats preparing for the first rush to St. Paul when word was received that the river was open.

Being the first steamboat into St. Paul was a major event each spring and good for business for the respective steamboat owners. The aggressive steamboat owners and equally aggressive Captain decided that the Lady Franklin would press on to the next pair of major river landings; La Crosse, La Crosse County, Wisconsin or Winona, Winona County, Minnesota. After a brief stop to refuel and with the recent late February warm weather in mind, eager immigrant passengers on board, and a load of valuable cargo, the Lady Franklin pressed on.

Around April 3, 1856 and in the vicinity of Alma, Buffalo County, Wisconsin, the Lady Franklin encountered ice. Lake Pepin was still frozen over and the steamboat could not continue. Because of the warm weather, the crew and passengers did not think the delay would be long. There was a river travel practice that when a river steamboat would breakdown or otherwise be unable to continue, it would tie up to the nearest shore and the passengers would debark and fend for themselves. Usually the passengers would get accommodations in the nearest river town or campout along the shore. The Lady Franklin did just that and tied up to the shore. It is not known if she tied up on the Wisconsin shore or the Minnesota shore. Because of lack of accommodations or a desire save their limited funds, Diedrich and his family found themselves setting up a rustic camp along the river. It is likely that Casper Klinkhammer, Henry Berger, and the Joseph Toenjes and Henry Witschen families also camped nearby. The men scrounged the nearby fields for food, getting some from Lady Franklin provisions and buying everything else from the local population.

The short delay turned into two very long weeks! The experience was probably a valuable learning experience for when the families first settled on their own land. While tied up, the crew of the Lady Franklin purchased wood and some other supplies from the local citizens to replenish the steamboat.

Sometime during the days of April 16 or 17, 1856, it was decided that the ice had melted enough to attempt moving up river. After everyone embarked, the Lady Franklin headed for Red Wing, Minnesota Territory. There must have been a shipboard celebration when the Lady Franklin successfully navigated Lake Pepin and entered the main channel of the Mississippi River. After a short run, Lady Franklin tied up to the Red Wing levee. The town of Red Wing was small but a growing and an important refueling station for the riverboats.

After a quick refueling in Red Wing, the Lady Franklin pushed hard and arrived in St. Paul April 18, 1856. It was the first steamboat to arrive that season and the ship, crew, and passengers received a rousing welcome from the city's citizens. The Gohman family must have felt very welcome and likely joined in the celebration.

Final Trek; Coming Home

St. Paul was a booming metropolis by 1856 and quite accustomed to the influx of German Immigrants arriving on the steamboats. Merchants, teamsters and, yes, even shysters were readily available to either help or take advantage of the new arrivals. Fort St. Anthony, now known as Fort Snelling, was established in 1819 at the confluence of the Mississippi and Minnesota rivers. In 1838, about 5 miles (8.0 km) downstream and on the north bank of the river, a new settlement was started. It was known as "L'Oeil de Cochon" or "Pig's Eye". In 1841, Father Lucien Galtier renamed the settlement St. Paul. When the Minnesota Territory was formalized in 1849, St. Paul was named its capital. In 1854, St. Paul incorporated as a city and in 1858, Minnesota became the 32nd state. Natural geography and location led to St. Paul becoming a trade and transportation center. By 1856, it had become a gateway to the Minnesota frontier and the Dakota Territory. From St. Paul, settlers could take established trails all the way to the Red River Valley. The series of trails became known as the Red River Trails. One of the later developed trails was known as the "East Plains Trail" or the "Saint Anthony Trail" depending on the direction one was traveling. It followed older routes out of St. Paul, along the river to St. Cloud and Sauk Rapids, across the upper valleys of several Minnesota River tributaries, through Breckenridge, Minnesota, and on to Pembina, in what is now North Dakota and the Red River Valley.

St. Paul circa 1856 waterfront

After a quick look around St. Paul, Diedrich made arrangements for his family to be transported to Sauk Rapids which was further upstream on the east bank of the Mississippi. It was the location of the federal Sauk River Land District Office and where Diedrich wanted to inquire about land available for claiming. The office was opened when the Sauk River Land District was created in 1852. Diedrich could have arranged for seats on a stagecoach that ran to the St. Cloud area, across from Sauk Rapids. However, it is more likely he arranged transportation with an oxcart owner-driver to take the family and its few belongings over the unfamiliar trail. Family tradition also indicates the use of oxen pulled cart or wagon. Departing the big city, the Gohmann family left for the area of their new home.

Traveling about two miles an hour or about ten miles a day, the ox cart, with the Gohman family often walking along side, took nearly a week to arrive in Sauk Rapids. Diedrich's first order of business was to find a place to bed down. Family tradition indicated it was in the local church. The church, only rarely used by itinerant priests, was largely unattended and vacant. It was very likely a refuge for weary travelers. A couple weeks later, two Benedictine Priests, Fathers Demetrius and Cornelius, were also known to have lived there a short time until other accommodations could be arranged.

Diedrich's next order of business was to visit the Sauk River Land District office. It was easy to find as it was the most important office in town. After arriving at the land office, Diedrich showed his warrant and was provided information about the land that had been made available for sale, claiming, possible to "locate a warrant on", or otherwise unoccupied. Most the unclaimed land was in newly created but yet un-organized Stearns County, one of the nine counties, at the time, in the Minnesota Territory. Just over a year ago, the land had been considered "Indian Territory". The land had not yet been formally surveyed by the federal government and most of the land was not yet made available for sale or to "locate a warrant on". The land office federal Receiver and/or federal Register would point out land that had already been claimed by "squatting". Some claimed land such as the future sites of several towns including St. Augusta had been locally surveyed. The first survey of St. Augusta had been done in 1855. Aware of the location of land available for acquisition, Diedrich likely went afield by himself to check out the land.

> *One family tradition has it that Diedrich built a dugout canoe and used it to visit the new land, returning to get the family. For many reasons, that is extremely unlikely. Like everyone visiting the federal Sauk River Land District Office concerning homesteads on the other side of the river, Diedrich had better options.*

In 1856, there was a surprising amount of traffic between Sauk Rapids and St. Cloud that had to cross the river. One option Diedrich had, but the less likely, was an area in the river that was commonly forded during low water levels. It was in the area of what is modern day St. Cloud's Hester Park. Those that used it were usually on horseback or owned their own high wheeled wagons. Diedrich may have crossed on foot but it is unlikely he later brought the family that way. There were also three nearby ferries operating between the east and west banks of the river which had been established the year before.

Diedrich, and later with his family, likely used one of the ferry services between Sauk Rapids and St. Cloud. Most probable and mentioned in one early Gohmann story, he used a ferry with a western terminal at a location known as the St. Germain Ferry Landing. Some St. Cloud histories erroneously report that the ferry was owned by Anthony Edelbrock. In fact, it was owned by John L. Wilson but operated by Mr. Edelbrock's son. John Wilson built one of the very first log cabins in St. Cloud and Anthony Edelbrock was the first to bring a family with when settling in St. Cloud. The Edelbrock family arrived sometime during 1854. John Wilson and Anthony Edelbrock also had several other business relationships. The Edelbrock family went on to be proprietors of several well-known St. Cloud businesses. Shortly after the Gohman family arrival in the area, a contingent of Benedictine Priests also arrived and used the ferry numerous times. The Edelbrock son became close to the priests and he eventually joined them and became Abbot Alexius Edelbrock, OSB of what is now St. John's Abbey.

Crossing the river, Diedrich found himself in the new city of St. Cloud. The month earlier, March 1856, three towns, known as Upper, Middle, and Lower towns were incorporated as a single city, St. Cloud. Upper Town, also known as Arcadia, was plotted by General Sylvanus Lowry, a slaveholder and trader from Kentucky who had brought slaves with him. He served as St. Cloud's first mayor in 1856. Almost all of the Southerners left Upper town when the Civil War broke out. However, Lowry died there in 1865. Middle Town was mostly settled by Catholic German immigrants from the Eastern United States; many via Cincinnati. Lower Town was primarily populated by settlers who came from Northeastern United States.

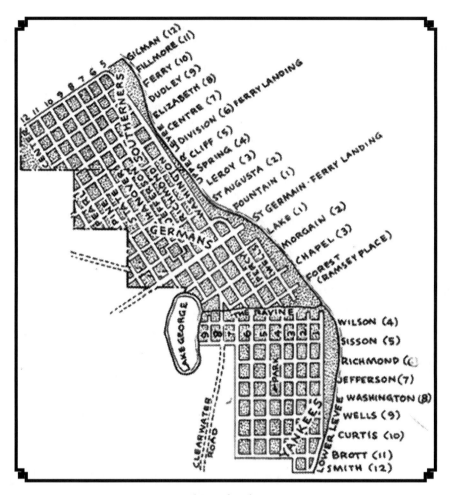

1856 St. Cloud Map

After making his way down the primitive road, known as the Clearwater Road, which followed the Mississippi southward through the area where St. Augusta was being developed, Diedrich discovered the land of his dreams. He had to create a verifiable description of the land he had chosen. Three methods were in use at the time. First, was using natural and manmade landmarks that were thought likely to not change much over time such as shores of waterways, bluffs, rock out-cropping's, roads, and similar things immediate visible and obvious to the eye. Second, was to mark the perimeter corners with obelisks, usually visible piles of rock or other materials thought to be permanent. The third was to identify a center point and to claim some quantity of the surrounding acreage. Diedrich likely used some combination of all three.

Federal laws governing expansion into newly acquired areas such as the Louisiana Purchase had made it unlawful to claim the surveyed land by simply occupying it. Later acts such as the Pre-emption Act of September 1841 gave pre-emptive rights to early settlers of specific areas. An 1854 federal land act extended the pre-emption rights to early settlers of un-surveyed Minnesota Territory. By filing an intention to purchase with the responsible land district, the settler or pre-emptor could protect the claim by committing to purchase it later at a minimum price of $1.25 per acre. Returning to Sauk Rapids and the Sauk River Land District Office, Diedrich presented his warrant and declared his intent to "locate the warrant" which could satisfy the purchase commitment. The federal Receiver, William H. Hood, entered Diedrich's transaction for 120 acres into the record and the federal Register, George W. Sweet, accepted the necessary payments and issued receipts for the transaction. The usual fees for an intent or temporary claim transaction was a filing fee of $10.00 and a $2.00 commission paid to the office agents. Very early intent and town filings resulted in the claim or proposed town being shown on the surveyed published in 1857. Since Diedrich's filing took place simultaneous with the actual survey of the land, his and like claims are not shown. A careful study of the Sauk Rapids/St. Cloud Land Office records held by the Minnesota Historical Society might reveal the actual transaction.

During the first few days of May 1856, Diedrich and family crossed the Mississippi River and made their way to their new homestead.

Homestead Life

The Diedrich Gohmann homestead was located along the west bank of the Mississippi River. Later after it was surveyed and in future land patent documents, it was described as the "Southwest Quarter of South West Quarter; the lot no. One of Section eight and the Lot no. four of Section Seventeen in Township one hundred and twenty three; North of Range Twenty Seven, West; containing one hundred and twenty acres". (SW 1/4 of the SW 1/4, and Lot 1 in Section 8 and part of Lot 4 in section 17, all in TWP123N, Range 27W).

> *One early Family story was that The Gohman family had arrived in 1854 or 1855 and lived for a brief time in a cave on the site of what was to become the original St. Augusta site. Another Family story was that the family arrived in 1856 and came directly to the homestead site. That first story was partially the result of details in the Gohman land patent or deed. That story is not possible. Diedrich appeared in the Court of Common Pleas in Cincinnati October 9, 1854, to finalize his citizenship and it would have been too late to still get to the St. Augusta area much less survive the winter unprepared. The next spring, the first steamboat did not get to St. Paul until April 17th which is after the family's supposed occupancy of the St. Augusta site in March. Also river travelers were not surprised that spring by a frozen Lake Pepin. A little later in this Chapter, why the land patent contained incorrect information will be explained. Also, spring 1856 when the family did arrive, the St. Augusta site had already been claimed and surveyed.*

Early Years

May 1856, Diedrich built a temporary lean-to shelter, and then set about getting a garden grubbed and planted before the growing season got too far along. Their very survival hinged on getting the food from that garden. The temporary lean-to shelter has been described as being a frame of "dried popular branches covered with hay". Living their dream started with a challenge.

One Family story tells that Diedrich paid $50.00 for a cow and a calf leaving him with fifty cents to face the rest of the year. The story was also in a newspaper story about the Golden Wedding Anniversary of one of Diedrich's sons. At the time, farm animals were scarce, in high demand, and extremely costly. For $50.00, he could also have bought another forty acres from neighboring settlers.

The big news during the families first month in the St. Augusta area was the arrival in St. Cloud of one large group and one small group of new settlers. A large group of immigrants known as the "German Colony" arrived on May 9, 1856 followed by five Benedictine priests arriving May 21, 1856. Diedrich and his family had established themselves on land just days before the new immigrants arrived; many of whom also claimed land in the St. Augusta area.

October 17, 1856, the Gohman family welcomed a new son, John Diedrick Gohman. Hearing of the birth, Fr. Cornelius Wittman came by horseback to baptize the boy. Fr. Cornelius had arrived in the area about the same time as the Gohman family and was one of the priests who started St. John's Abbey. He also went on to found several churches and schools in the surrounding area. He was well loved as a priest and a teacher. Fr. Cornelius' birthday was October 15th just two days before the new baby's. While visiting the family and observing how little shelter they had, Fr. Cornelius urged Diedrich to quickly build a better shelter for the family before winter arrived with any ferocity.

Heeding the advice of Fr. Cornelius and with the garden harvested, the family put their backs into building a better home. It may have been a cave dug into the side of a hill or a small log cabin. Most likely it was a combination of both, a dugout. The dugout could have been a hole in the ground with a flat roof covered by logs and ground. This dugout was probably dug into the hillside with a built out log front and a log and sod roof. The early pioneers often built such dugouts as a shelter for both man and beast. The winter of 1856 – 1857 was uncommonly cold. A sustained period of -25° F was recorded at Fort Snelling, miles to the south. At least one reading of -43 ° F was also recorded. The bad weather continued through a cold and wet May. Fr. Cornelius' advice was timely and the dugout kept the family safe even if uncomfortable.

Dugout house typical of those in use

The Surveyor General's Office of Iowa and Wisconsin began the first government land survey of a portions of the Minnesota Territory in 1848. The survey was conducted with the idea of subdividing the land and selling it to settlers. The Office of Surveyor General of Minnesota was created in early 1857, a year before statehood. Its mission was to complete the survey of the rest of Minnesota. The survey was a slow and difficult process and it took until 1907 to complete. During the spring and summer of 1856, the surveyors were working the area that encompassed the Diedrich Gohmann plat. April 16, 1857, that portion of the survey was accepted and published.

Despite the unusually cold winter, a plague of grasshoppers continued after beginning late the previous year. Despite Mother Nature's challenges, Diedrich and the family continued to clear their land and plant crops. The rudimentary tools they had available made the work slow and tedious but they persevered.

The family participated in a survey of the area inhabitants. That survey later became known as the 1857 Minnesota Territory Township 123 Census Record.

A new market for the homestead's crops opened during February 1858. The N.N. Smith grist mill began operation making flour of locally grown wheat and corn. It was the first grist mill in Stearns County.

By 1858, the Sauk River Land District had become more commonly called the St. Cloud Land District. April 19th of that year, the district office moved from Sauk Rapids to St. Cloud and the district renamed. The new office opened for business April 29, 1858. The following month, May 11, 1858, Minnesota Territory became the 32nd state of the United States of America.

It is not certain exactly when, but Diedrich began building a new home for the family. Most of the settlers in the area were building square homes but Diedrich built one rectangular, about 16 feet by 20 feet. Like many of his neighbors, the new house had a loft that was accessible by a ladder. The loft was used as a sleeping space for the children and for storage. In a later description, no mention was made of the number of rooms so it is likely the main floor was a single large room with an exterior door and two windows. Family elders have reported the house was built of logs. A short time later it was covered with "clap boards" to appear like newer homes being built of locally sawn boards. Beginning in late 1855, the demand for boards led to sawmills being brought in during 1856 and operations begun in both the lower-town part of St. Cloud and in nearby St. Augusta. Eventually after several generations of property owners, the wood used in the original homestead home was used for firewood to heat the current home.

May 31, 1859, another son, Joseph Gohman, is born to the family. He was a welcome addition and as he grew older would be able to contribute his brawn to the expanding farm effort. Later that summer a tornado ripped through the Town of St. Augusta and destroyed everything in its path. It is not known how the Gohman family faired during the tornadoes near miss of their property. For the next couple of years, the residents of the town organized and reorganized under various names.

Early 1860, Diedrich began to be concerned about how secure his ownership of the homestead land was. A number of things were possible issues; the 1857 survey, no written land patent, and news of on-going court battles over the validity and use of military land warrants. Also the news of the proposed sale of surveyed federal lands in the St. Cloud Land District was being transmitted across the country. The uncertainty resulted in a great many letters and other correspondence originating from the St. Cloud District Land Office. *The Minnesota Historical Society holds many examples of them.* Many were written to the Commissioner of the General Land Office. Other letters were sent to federal and state officials plus some to private citizens holding claims. The letters often addressed matters relating to imperfect or contested entries (with considerable detail about the claimant and improvements made to the land in question). The letters to claimants consisted primarily of notices of action, requests for information, and procedural instructions. In general the letters addressed homestead and preemption claims, military bounty entries, other land grants and script based claims. The uncertainty was sweeping across the settlers of the entire area first known as Stevens County and then Stearns County. A great deal of fear was generated.

The 1857 survey of the area meant that all the claimed or purchased plots would have to be realigned to fit the legal descriptions established by the survey. Such realignments would take time and a great deal of diplomacy and negotiation.

Two issues concerning the purchase and use of military warrants were resulting in court battles across the country. First, was over the legality of reassigning (selling) the rights to a land warrant presented as a military benefit. To this day, anyone having served in the military cannot reassign future military earnings or benefits. Second, concerned the clause in the respective laws governing the issuance of the warrants that indicated they could only be used for federally surveyed land. The Gohman family's land had not been surveyed at the time they settled on it.

Unknown to Diedrich, May 1, 1860 the Peter Hollis warrant reassignment was accepted as valid in the St. Paul, Minnesota District Land Office. Also unknown is why it was processed there instead of the St. Cloud District Land Office.

Because of his concerns over ownership of the homestead land and his 1856 intent filing, Diedrich joined many other Stearns County settlers and filed a homestead claim June 26, 1860 using all possible methods. Land could be acquired from the federal land office by directly purchasing for cash at a land auction, a claim under the Pre-emption Act of September 1841, a claim under one of the other homestead acts, and the "location" of a previously issued military warrant. As others in the land district were doing, Diedrich filed under two of the four possible filings. He filed under the Pre-emption Act of September 1841 to prove his claim to the land and using the original Hollis warrant which he submitted with his application to pay the required $1.25 an acre for the land.

The Pre-emption Act permitted "squatters" who were living on federal government owned land to purchase up to 160 acres at a price not less than $1.25 per acre. To qualify under the law, the "squatter" had to be a "head of household" or a single man over 21 or a widow. They had to be a citizen of the United States or an immigrant who had declared intent to become a naturalized citizen. They also had to be a resident of the claimed land for a minimum of 14 months. To preserve ownership, the claimant had to actively reside on the land and/or improve the land for a minimum of five years. The land could not be idle for any six month period. After meeting those requirements a final land patent would be issued.

Many other Stearns County settlers found themselves in the same predicament as Diedrich. There were so many filing a claim under the Pre-emption Act that a hand written form was developed by the St. Cloud Land District office and was used by all. The form detailed carefully how the claimant met each prerequisite of the Act, real and perceived as being required. Blanks were left in the form for the claimant to complete. The form went so far as to even partially describe the home that was built on the property. The form even assumed that homes were all square!

In Diedrich's filing, his status as a married head of household and his age is stated. It is interesting that his Naturalization Intent document was attached to the filing rather than his final Naturalization Document. It may be an example of what the perceived requirement was and not the actual requirement or the final document may not have been available. Each piece of property was identified using the 1857 survey description and how it was improved for five years and never allowed to be idle. Diedrich's filing had the home being square crossed out and included the description of the Gohman home as being:

> "20 ft by 16 ft and 1 ½ story high and has a good roof and floor and contains one door and two windows and is a comfortable house for a family to live in and has lived in and made it is exclusive home from the first day of May, 1855 till the present time".

During the stated May, 1855, the Gohman family was still in Cincinnati. Those filing secondary claims with St. Cloud Land District office were all under the misperception that they had to have been on the land and improving it for five years. Actually, they only had to reside on the land for 14 months and improving the land with the intent that the improvement period would be five years. After which the final patent would be issued. A great many of the claims filed in the District during the time that Diedrich filed contain examples of similar exaggeration, especially the time the land was under improvement. Although Diedrich's filing record doesn't include one, most of the filings also included a required affidavit signed by two neighbors that the claims were correct. The claimants were doing what they thought had to be done to protect their land. The St. Cloud Land Office officials had to know the claimed residing times were exaggerations. Some of the earliest dates being claimed occurred when the land was still held by the Indians. It is also obvious from the application form prepared by the St. Cloud Land Office that newly appointed federal Register, Joel D. Cruttenden, and Recorder, Samuel E. Adams, were ready to accept claims despite those exaggerations. The fee for filing these documents was usually $6.00.

The use of various spellings of the Gohman surname became an issue during the filing of the land claim. Diedrich was required to submit a declaration that clarified and attested to his surname.

In effect, Diedrich was paying for his land at $1.25 an acre with the warrant that he had bought earlier for an unknown amount of money. The price he paid covered all the land covered by his warrant plus a $1.25 an acre for some land in excess of the warrant's 120 acres. Again, there are many examples of this happening to other settlers in the St. Cloud Land Office area.

July 14, 1860 brought the census taker to the Gohman household. It was the first regular federal census taken in the new state of Minnesota and enumerated all the members of a household as of June 1, 1860.

September 23, 1861, another son is born to the family, Frank Jerome Gohman. He was another welcome addition to the family.

1862 brought more excitement and fear to the Gohman family with the beginning of the Dakota War of 1862 also known as the Sioux Uprising. It was an armed conflict between the United States and several bands of the Eastern Sioux or Eastern Dakota as they were also known. It began on August 17, 1862, along the Minnesota River in southwest Minnesota. While primarily focused in southwestern Minnesota, further north the Sioux attacked several unfortified stagecoach stops and river crossings along the Red River Trails, including the "East Plains Trail" / "Saint Anthony Trail" which included the St. Cloud area. Mail carriers, stage drivers and military couriers were killed while attempting to reach settlements as far flung as Pembina, North Dakota and St. Cloud, Minnesota. Two safe havens were built in St. Cloud to provide security for its inhabitants. One was in a large building in the middle-town area and a military fort known as Fort Holes in the lower-town area of St. Cloud. The residents did not use the fort during the uprising but it did accommodate people coming in from the outlying areas. The Gohman family and their neighbors had to temporarily abandon their homesteads and flee to St. Cloud, perhaps even crossing the Mississippi. A Gohman family story relates:

> "When John D., was seven years old the family was driven off its farm by Indians, then on the warpath. They went by ox cart to the Sauk Rapids ferry to get away from the Indian raids. On what is now Reformatory hill they met the Union Soldiers. It was three weeks before the family was able to safely return home."

The Sioux Uprising officially ended with the execution of 38 Dakota men on December 26, 1862, in Mankato, Minnesota.

During 1863 and 1864, the Gohman family experienced a severe drought and their fields and gardens suffered. A wonderful break from worrying about the drought came when a daughter, Anna Maria Elizabeth Gohman, was born July 7, 1864.

On November 20, 1864, a land patent was finally signed awarding Johann Diedrich Gohmann the land he had worked so long and hard for. Sometime later, St. Cloud Land District Office federal Register, Thomas McClure, or Receiver, Charles Gilman, notified Diedrich that the patent was in place and his concerns about the future were relieved.

The birth of Stephen Gohman is celebrated February 1, 1867. Apparently, later that spring the Gohman family had to leave the homestead due to flooding. A Family story relates:

> "When John D., was eleven years old the family was again forced to leave its home, this time because high water in the Mississippi River."

There is no official record of the Mississippi River flooding in 1867 but, in nearby St. Paul, 10 inches of rain was recorded in a very short time. Also, about the middle of July, western parts of the Sauk River had a single cloudburst that caused major flooding. Bridges were washed away in central Stearns County. The deluge of water from the Sauk River into the Mississippi is likely what disrupted the Gohmann's life. It was something that happened periodically because of river flooding. It was the sediment deposited by these very floods that made the Gohman homestead soil so rich and productive.

On April 28, 1867, the awarded land patent was recorded in the Stearns County, Minnesota book of deeds. June 6, 1867, the Gohmann family joined the parishioners of St. Mary Help of Christians Catholic Church as they celebrated the arrival of a 1,600 pound bell for their church steeple.

Later Years

Tragedy visited the Gohman family when the Matriarch died November 10, 1869. The cause of death was given as "Congestion of the Brain". Maria Elisabeth (Börger) Gohmann had crossed the Atlantic Ocean, traversed a large part of the United States, helped create a thriving homestead, and bore nine children with all but one surviving. She truly deserved the title of Matriarch. Shortly after her death, Elisabeth was buried in the burial ground of the original St. Augusta Catholic Church.

After the death of his cherished wife, Diedrich pulled off a remarkable feat. After burying his wife the second week of November 1869, Diedrich made arrangements for support of the children. He put the older children in charge of the homestead and traveled to Cincinnati. Once there, he got married again. Diedrich managed to return home in time for the spring planting and was listed, June 23, 1870, in an important national census. Diedrich's first wife, Maria Elisabeth was also enumerated in a special 1870 census listing all who died the previous year.

Diedrich must have been fortunate enough to have gotten passage on a steamboat out of St. Paul just before the Mississippi River froze over and then an early passage for him and his new wife on one of the first steamboats to leave Cincinnati in the spring. Much of the rest of this feat is left to the reader's imagination but Diedrich's Brother, Johann Heinrich Gohman, may have served as matchmaker.

Diedrich and Gertrud Gohmann's
church marriage record excerpt

January 1, 1870, Diedrich married, Gertrud Hegemann, at St. Augustine Catholic Church in Cincinnati, Hamilton County, Ohio. Her given name was always recorded without an "e". Gertrud had been born May 27, 1826 in Lünebach, Bitburg-Prum, Rheinland-Pfalz, Germany. She was baptized at the Saint Felizitas Catholic Church in Lünebach. Her parents were Anton and Catherina Elisabet (Jaspers) Hegemann. At age 43, Gertrud could have been either a Cincinnati widow or a spinster before her marriage. There is some evidence that she may have been previously married but the records are inconclusive.

With the spring ice breakup, Diedrich and Gertrud hurried back to the family homestead in St. Augusta. There, Gertrud worked to earn the trust and confidence of the eight Gohman children and to assume the role of Mother. A step-grandchild remembers their parent telling how good Gertrud was to her new step-children.

The Gohman family participated in the 1870 National Census. They were counted June 23, 1870 but the data collected reflected a place of residence on June 1, 1870. In many ways, this census had special significance; enumerators were required to number the records according to the order in which they visited each residence, birthdays were recorded in a more accurate way, ages were recorded as fractions, sex, color, profession, real estate ownership, literacy level and mental and physical competency levels were also recorded. It was also the first census to document parental birth places and immigrant status plus Civil War survivorship. The census even included an agriculture schedule that revealed the Gohman homestead included 30 acres of improved land, 80 acres of woodland, and had an estimated value of $2,000 for the land and equipment. Diedrich had 2 horses, 3 milk cows, 5 pigs, and 5 other cattle for a total estimated value of $500. The estimated 1870 production included 200 bushels of wheat, 300 bushels of corn, 15 pounds of wool, 50 pounds of butter, 6 tons of hay and some potatoes for a total estimated value of $414. The estimated value of animals being sold to slaughter was $140 for a total production estimate of $554. Obviously, Diedrich's recent five months away from the farm to marry a new wife did not hurt his farm's production.

During 1873, the Town of St. Augusta moved about a mile west of its original location on the Mississippi River. There is disagreement amongst historians about the reason for the move. One scenario is the people moved because of the regular spring floods. The other scenario is that the St. Mary Help of Christians Catholic Church building became too small and the congregation began building a bigger church a mile west. During the construction, Diedrich and his sons, along with other parishioners, worked together to build the new church. Fr. Valentine Stimmler guided the construction. The businesses of the town then followed and relocated near the church. Soon after and because of the flooding, remains in the original cemetery were exhumed and moved to a new cemetery adjacent to the new church building. The remains of the Gohman Matriarch, Maria Elisabeth (Börger) Gohmann, were moved during the process.

Maria Elisabeth (Börger) Gohmann's tombstone

The Gohman family experienced one of the coldest winters in recorded history during 1874–1875. To the south, Fort Snelling's average temperature during January and February was well below zero Fahrenheit. Many shallowly dug wells froze up; leaving those homesteads without water. Several homesteaders lost their homes to fires as the residents attempted to stay warm. The winter during the Gohman's first year, 1856-1857, and this one were harbingers of things to come. Some warmth came to the family during 1875 when the oldest son, John Bernard "Barney" Gohman, married Katherine "Kate" Mund.

The Gohman family enjoyed hearing the news about the world around them. 1876 brought them news about the celebrations of the 100 year anniversary of the founding of the United States and the battle of the "Little Big Horn" or "Custer's Last Stand". Closer to home, they heard about the infamous James and Younger brothers robbing a Northfield, Minnesota bank and escaping.

Despite a dry spring, the summer of 1878 produced magnificent fields of crops. While bringing in the bountiful harvest, the Gohman family's happiness turned to sorrow when another tragedy befell them. Their third youngest child, Frank Jerome Gohman, died September 15, 1878.

February 2, 1879, Diedrich and Gertrud executed a bill of sale transferring the original Gohman homestead to his son and her stepson, John Diedrich Gohman, for the sum of $1,500. The bill of sale was notarized April 9, 1879. Diedrich and Gertrude continued to live on the homestead and are listed in the next census as residing in the household of John and Mary Gohman.

1880-1881 snowfall

The winter of 1880–1881 became widely known as the most severe winter ever experienced in the United States. The snow began arriving during October 1880 and blizzard after blizzard followed throughout the winter, well into March 1881. The Gohman homestead was snowbound throughout the entire winter. Roads were blocked and railroads and steamboats were at a standstill. Minnesota cities became desperate for supplies. The October blizzard brought snow so deep that almost the entire first floor of the Gohman home was inundated. It is unknown if the Gohman family had completed the fall harvest and were prepared for the harsh winter. With no winter thaws and another huge blizzard which began February 2, 1881, the Gohman family had to dig tunnels between the house and out buildings to care for the livestock. It became necessary to dig openings in the snow to clear chimneys and to get air into the house and animal shelters. Even for farmers such as the Gohmans, food and fuel began to run out. When the snow finally melted in late spring, the Gohman land flooded again. Downstream in the more central and southern states, the high water of the Missouri and Mississippi rivers flooded vast areas of the river plains. Laura Ingalls Wilder related her experiences during this winter in her book "The Long Winter".

The Patriarch of the Gohman family died, Monday, July 11, 1887 at age 73. He was memorialized as a "religious, thrifty man not deterred by hard work". He was buried in the St. Mary Help of Christians Cemetery in St. Augusta, July 13, 1887. A church death record entry provided the date of burial and the name of his parents; Diedrich and Adelaide Gohmann.

Diedrich Gohmann's obituary

81

Diedrich's obituary translates as follows "The ranks of the pioneers in St. Augusta have again thinned out further. On Monday afternoon Herr Johann D. Gohmann died at the advanced age of 73. He had been continuously ill in recent years. Fortified with the healing strength of the Catholic religion, and entrusting himself to the power of the Lord over life and death, he took leave of mortal life. Yesterday morning the burial took place attended by the members of the community. Thirty-two years ago the deceased came to St. Augusta at a time when everything there was still wilderness. He belongs to those industrious farmers who would never allow any difficulty to thwart them in winning the fruits of the earth. At his grave he was mourned by his wife together with seven grown children. To them our sympathy and to him eternal rest."

After Diedrich's death, Gertrud, continued to live with Diedrich's fifth child, John Diedrich Gohman and his wife, Mary.

A huge blizzard and white-out surprised Minnesota, January 12, 1888. It was not safe to leave shelter during the storm. Two hundred thirty five people died in the storm; most of them children. As a result, it became known as the "School House Blizzard of 1888". Gertrud was relieved when it was over and, fortunately, all the Gohman family was accounted for.

Christmas Eve, 1899, Gertrud died and was buried Christmas Day in the St. Mary Help of Christians Cemetery. Her death brought an end to the Gohman family immigrant era.

Diedrich and Gertrud Gohmann's Tombstone
was placed at a later date

The Matriarch and Patriarch created a Gohman family that can be best described by a statement made by the Russian writer Alexander Solzhenitsyn.

> "The German is like a willow. No matter which way you bend him, he will always take root again."

John Bernard Gohman and Katherine Mund

John Bernard Gohman and Katherine Mund

John Bernard "Barney" Gohman was born Sunday, April 4, 1847, in Cincinnati, Hamilton County, Ohio. He was the first child of what was to become the dynasty of the new family patriarch, Johann Diedrich Gohmann, and the new matriarch, Maria Elisabeth (Börger) Gohmann. He was baptized the next day, April 5, 1847, at St. John the Baptist Catholic Church in Cincinnati. The service was conducted by Fr. William Unterthiemer. His godparents were John Bernard Börger and Elisabeth Homann; possibly a misspelling of Gohmann. Many think Elisabeth was either his mother's sister or half-sister. John Bernard was also known as Bernard and became commonly called Barney.

His first years were spent in the large bustling city of Cincinnati where there was much to observe and learn. By the time he was six, Barney was expected to help care for his younger siblings and to do some household chores. As a nine year old, Barney experienced the thrilling adventure of a steamboat trip down the Ohio and up the Mississippi rivers to a new frontier homeland in the Minnesota Territory. He spent much of his shipboard time playing with the two oldest Toenjes children, Mary and Joseph. Barney was about the same age as Mary and a year older than Joseph. The shipboard life plus short stopovers in river towns and cities brought new opportunities to observe and learn. From that experience on the river, it was "in his blood".

For the next sixteen years, he helped his father, Diedrich, build and farm a homestead in a new land and grew into manhood. From "grubbing" the earth for the first time to expanding the land one owned, Barney came to love the land. Along the way, Barney learned from his parents that perseverance, thrift, and hard work paid off. Family and land became the two things that Barney cherished most.

During those same sixteen years, Barney experienced Minnesota becoming the 32nd U.S. state, the American Civil War, and the Sioux uprising. He observed the economic changes brought by improved logging and farming methods plus the development of national and regional railroads.

An Andrew Parker received a military patent, number 777, for 160 acres. He sold the patent to a Charles Wilson who claimed 160 acres in the St. Cloud Land District. The property was described as "Southeast quarter of Section 18, Township 123 North, Range 27 West, consisting of 160 acres". Wilson sold the land to Henry Schlagbeck May 15, 1866. He, in turn, sold 80 acres of the land to Barney October 1, 1872 for $475.00. April 5, 1875, Barney sold the 80 acres to his brother, Henry for $500.00. The land was now described as "South half of the Southeast quarter of Section 18 in Township 123 North, Range 27 West, containing 80 acres". A notice in the local paper April 8, 1875 reported the sale.

John Bernard "Barney" Gohman married Katherine "Kate" Mund in 1875 in St. Augusta, Stearns County, Minnesota. The exact date of the marriage is unknown but they likely married between April 8, 1875 and May 6, 1875, two land transfer dates. Katherine was born July 11, 1851 in Cologne, North Rhine-Westphalia, Germany to Wilhelm and Cecelia Mund. Her mother's maiden name was spelled Gey, Grey, or Guy. Katherine was commonly called Kate. She had been married earlier to Arthur August Hilsgen and had two children with him, Peter and Anthony. August passed away shortly after the birth of his second son in 1871. The second son, Anthony, died in 1875.

May, 6, 1875, the local paper published an announcement concerning the purchase of 16 acres for $150.00 by Barney and Kate from Kate's father. They started farming in a small way. Sometime later, Barney laid claim to eighty acres under the Homestead Act of 1862. Barney is the only child known to follow in his father's footsteps by acquiring farmland through homesteading. Barney received a homestead deed to the property July 20, 1881. The land was described as "east half of the southwest quarter of section thirty in township one hundred and twenty three north of range twenty-seven west of the Fifth Principal Meridian in Minnesota".

About the time Barney was acquiring his farm land, there was a developing market demand for fresh fruit. For about the next ten years, surrounding farmers began experimenting with growing apples, plums, and several types of berries. Between unscrupulous tree and seed vendors, bad weather, and lack of knowledge; most experiments did not go well. Like the other Gohmans, Barney experimented a bit with fruit production but settled on more consistent grain and general farming. Local farmers, including Barney, experienced a particularly rainy fall in 1899. During the first 19 days of October over eight and one half inches fell. Nearly half of that was within a twenty four hour period.

A description of Barney included he was of medium build and height with either blue or green eyes and brown bushy hair and mustache. Barney called his mustache "his soup strainer". Kate's grandchildren described her as a kind and gentle person.

Barney and Kate produced a very large family including ten sons and five daughters. In birth order they were Gertrude, Anna Maria, William, John Diedrick, Henry Heinrich, Cecelia Elizabeth, Joseph Bernard, Christopher, Louis, Mary Katherine, Antonio Ludwig, Stephen Frank, Louis Bernard, Ida Cathryn, and Leo Alouysius. Family was very important to Barney and Kate. They took advantage of every opportunity to hold family gatherings.

Barney and Kate felt the pain of losing a child when Louis died right after birth in 1887, Antonio died when just twenty nine days old in 1889, and Cecelia Elizabeth (Gohman) Imholte died a tragic death in 1906.

September 17, 1910, Barney and Kate sold the homestead to their son, Christopher, for $3,000.00. It appears that Barney and Kate then moved to Clear Lake, Sherburne County.

Barney lost his wife and the children their dear mother when Kate died on Thursday, November 30, 1916, at St. Raphael Hospital in St. Cloud from internal hemorrhaging caused by a vehicle accident. The accident occurred earlier on a road near St. Joseph, Stearns County. She was buried on December 4, 1916, in the St. Mary Help of Christians Cemetery in St. Augusta. Local newspapers published stories and obituaries that contained erroneous information including dates, days, and even the name of the hospital.

Barney experienced the loss of another child when his daughter, Ida Cathryn (Gohman) Imholte died November 18, 1918 during the influenza epidemic.

The 1920 census lists Barney living in St. Cloud with his son, Stephen, and wife, Eva (Liesch) Gohman. Barney experienced the loss of two more children, John Diedrick during 1921 and Gertrude (Gohman) Beumer/Langanki during 1922.

Barney died June 23, 1923 from cardiac arrest and pneumonia. He died at home and his death certificate indicated he was residing back in Clear Lake. Barney was buried June 25, 1923 at St. Mary Help of Christians Cemetery in St. Augusta.

Barney and Kate Gohman's Tombstone

The Children of John Bernard "Barney" Gohman and Katherine "Kate" Mund

Gertrude (Gohman) Beumer/Langanki	(1877-1922)
Anna Maria (Gohman) Imholte	(1878-1929)
William Gohman	(1879-1935)
John Diedrick Gohman	(1881-1921)
Henry Heinrich Gohman	(1882-1950)
Cecelia Elizabeth (Gohman) Imholte	(1883-1906)
Joseph Bernard Gohman	(1885-1962)
Christopher Gohman	(1886-1957)
Louis Gohman	(1887-1887)
Mary Katherine (Gohman) Tschacher	(1888-1965)
Antonio Ludwig Gohman	(1889-1889)
Stephen Frank Gohman	(1890-1965)
Louis Bernard Gohman	(1892-1856)
Rose Mary Gohman	(1893-1972)
Ida Cathryn (Gohman) Imholte	(1895-1918)
Leo Alouysius Gohman	(1897-1980)

The Mund Family

Kate, her parents, and siblings immigrated to the United States via Antwerp, Belgium on the ship Sea Lark. They departed Antwerp on February 1, 1856 and arrived in New York on March 27, 1856. The family was not allowed to disembark for four days. They left the ship March 31, 1856. Kate's sister, Magdalene or Mary, appears to have been born on the voyage although the ship's manifest didn't reflect the birth or her passage. The manifest listed the family name as Mund although it was Mundt in Germany. As the family started their new life, they adopted the new name spelling.

Kate was the fourth of six children; Johann, Wilhelm, Gertrude, Kate, Magdalene, and Clara. The ship Sea Lark's manifest indicated a destination of Wisconsin and the family briefly stopped there before settling in Minnesota. They may have gone overland to Pittsburg, Allegheny County, Pennsylvania. From there, they would have traveled by riverboat down the Ohio River and then up the Mississippi to a river town in Wisconsin. Family tradition has the family arriving in Madison, Dane County, Wisconsin. If that is true, the family would have proceeded from New York to Madison by train on a newly opened railroad line. The same family tradition has it that they then went by ox cart to Sauk Rapids, Benton County, Minnesota. As Sauk Rapids was the area's district land office, Wilhelm would have gone there to start the homestead process. The family tradition goes on with a story that they forded the Mississippi river near the current Hester Park in St. Cloud. They also would have had the option of using the ferry that was operating full time between Sauk Rapids and St. Cloud.

Some newly arrived immigrants were organizing a group to create homesteads on land newly opened to settlement which was located southwest of St. Cloud. The Mund family quickly joined this group resulting in the first official record of the family in Minnesota, the 1857 Minnesota Territorial Census. The date of the actual census listing was October 22, 1857 and the family was listed living in Township 123, Range 28W, in Stearns County. Sometime before 1865, they relocated and made claim to a new homestead. That homestead was listed in the 1865 census as Fair Haven Township. In 1867, Luxemburg Township was formed and the homestead may have been part of the new township.

In his immigration documents, Kate's father, Wilhelm, declared his occupation as carpenter. After settling in Minnesota, he took up farming as did most of the other local German immigrants. His carpenter skills would come in handy as he built a home and farm buildings.

Kate's oldest brother, Johann, was born around 1844 in Germany. After settling in Minnesota, he married Catherine Richardson October 25, 1865 in the nearby small village of Luxemburg. After the marriage, Johann was more commonly known as John. Johann and Catherine began homesteading on 160 acres near Luxemburg and had six children; William, Josephus, Sarah, Elizabeth, Moritz, and Clara. They received a land patent dated November 13, 1884 but had left the land shortly after May 12, 1874. The land patent was cancelled January 29, 1886. Immediately after Clara's birth, the family had moved to an area known as St. Marks which is northwest of Wichita, Sedgwick County, Kansas. They then relocated to Andale, Sedgewick County which is further south. Johann died there in 1898 and Catherine also died there in 1911. Both were buried in St. Joseph Cemetery in Andale. Their youngest daughter, Clara, went on to marry Henry Ridder of Andale and eventually have 10 children, 60 grandchildren and 100 great-grandchildren.

The second oldest boy, Wilhelm, Jr., was born January 12, 1847 in Germany. He enlisted in the 11th Minnesota Infantry and served from April 12, 1864 to January 20, 1865. It is unlikely that he left Minnesota or saw any combat. Later in a special 1890 census of Military and Widows, his dates of service and his home in Fair Haven, for those dates, was confirmed. Wilhelm married Margaretha Rieschard April 17, 1866 in St. Augusta. A family memory is that Wilhelm and Margaretha also moved to Kansas with his brother, Johann, but returned to Minnesota in a very short time. They had eight children; John, Celia, Frank, Anne, another John, Elizabeth, Maggeret, and Peter. By the time of the 1910 census, Wilhelm and Margaretha had moved to the 1st Ward in St. Cloud. They both died there; her in 1916 and he in 1921. Both were buried in St. Mary Help of Christians Cemetery in St. Augusta.

By 1870, Kate and August Hilesen or Kate, the widow, would visit her parents, Wilhelm and Cecelia, who had left the family homestead and were living nearby in St. Augusta with Kate's sister, Gertrude, and her husband, Christopher Karls. Gertrude had been born in July 5, 1849, possibly in Cologne, Germany. By the time of the 1900 census, Gertrude and Christopher had sixteen children and eight were still alive. The known children include Theodore, William,

Nicolaus, Mathias, Lisi, Mary, Cecelia, Katharina, Elizabeth, Gertrude, Rosa, Anna, and Joseph. Christopher died between 1900 and 1910. Gertrude died September 30, 1925 in St. Cloud.

Later in 1885, Barney and Kate would have to travel to the home place of her brother, Wilhelm, Jr., to visit her parents. Wilhelm Jr. owned a Fair Haven homestead. The 1885 census indicated that Wilhelm and Cecelia had moved there and were living in a second residence that had been built. Her father, Wilhelm, died October 7, 1888 in Fair Haven. Family historians report that Kate's mother, Cecelia, remarried to H. Floyd and died 1898 in either Olmsted or Dakota counties. No documentation has been found to conclusively prove these scenarios. No records of her exist after the 1885 census. In 1904 Wilhelm, Jr. and his wife moved to St. Cloud, Stearns County. He died there June 23, 1947, most likely in St. Raphael's Hospital. His wife, Margaretha, died September 5, 1916.

Kate's second youngest sister, Magdalene is a bit of a mystery. She appears to have been born during the time that the family was immigrating to the United States. Perhaps even on the voyage across the Atlantic. However, the birth was not recorded in the ship's manifest. She is listed in the 1857 Minnesota census but not the one in 1865. Only one other record concerning Magdalene has been found. She is listed as Mary in a brief Mund family tree located in the LDS Church files. It is quite likely that she died between 1857 and 1865.

Kate's youngest sister, Clara, was living with her brother, Wilhelm, and family in 1870. She married John Mathias Scholtes April 13, 1873 in Wright County, Minnesota. After she married, Clara reverted to the use of Mundt as her maiden name. Clara and John had six children; Emma, Nicholas, Mae, Nora, Gertrude, and Jake. By the early 1900's, the Scholtes family had moved to California. Clara died December 12, 1931 in Burbank, Los Angeles County.

Katherine (Mund) Gohman (1851-1916) Family Recap

Parents:	William Mund	(1811-1888)
	Cecilia (Gey or Guy) Mund	(1817-1885)
Siblings:	Johann Mund	(1844-1898)
	Wilhelm Peter Mund	(1847-1921)
	Gertrude (Mund) Karls	(1849-1916)
	KATHERINE (MUND) GOHMAN	(1851-1916)
	Magdalene "Mary" Mund	(1856-?)
	Clara (Mund) Scholtes	(1858-1931)

Anna Marie Gohman and Henry Herman Berger

Anna Marie Gohman and Herman Henry Berger

Anna Marie Agnes Gohman was born Tuesday, April 17, 1849, in Cincinnati, Hamilton County, Ohio. She was the second child and first daughter of Patriarch, Diedrich, and Matriarch, Elisabeth, Gohman. The same day as her birth, Anna was baptized at St. John the Baptist Catholic Church in Cincinnati. Her Godparents were Henry Gohmann and Mary Agnes Börger. Henry was her uncle and Mary Agnes was likely her aunt. The presiding priest was Fr. Edmund Etschmann.

Just a young girl of seven, Anna accompanied her parents on a steamboat trip down the Ohio and up the Mississippi rivers to a home in the Minnesota Territory. It must have been a very exciting time for her as she and her brother, Barney, explored the steamboat and watched the deckhands at work. Traveling with the Gohmann family were Casper Klinkhammer, Henry Berger, and Joseph Toenjes and Henry Witschen families. Anna spent some shipboard time playing with the two youngest Toenjes children, Joseph and Henry. Anna was about the same age as Joseph and a year older than Henry. Anna and Henry Berger later married.

For the next eleven years, Anna experienced the hard work and drudgery associated with creating a new homestead in the wilderness. The oldest of three daughters, Anna assisted her mother with caring of the younger children and performing the household and garden chores. She also shared the experience of all homestead women when the difficulties of frontier life expanded their domain as they helped with farm work previously considered suitable only for men.

In 1862, Anna's father, Diedrich Gohmann sold forty acres located on the south side of the family homestead to Bernard Heinrich Dingmann and his wife. May 6, 1867, the Dingmanns sold that parcel to Henry Herman Berger. Henry was also homesteading 160 acres in nearby Section 26 of the township. "As the crow flies", the two parcels were slightly under four miles apart. Traveling between the two parcels took about an hour and a half to travel the six miles of roads that existed at the time.

Nine days later May 15, 1867, Henry married his new neighbor's daughter, Anna Marie Gohmann in St. Augusta, Stearns County, Minnesota at St. Mary's Help of Christians Catholic Church. A May-December marriage; Henry was 41 years old and Anna was 18. Witnesses at the wedding were Bernard Gohman and Maria Toenjes.

Henry was an imposing character. He obviously took great pride in looking and living the part of an adventurous outdoorsman.

Henry Herman Berger

Family tradition has it that after Henry was released from Civil War duties, he commanded a troop of Rangers that were sent to fight an Indian uprising in the Paynesville area of Stearns County. The same tradition has Henry losing an eye either during his Civil War or Indian uprising experiences.

Responding to the call for volunteers for frontier duty with the First Regiment of Mounted Rangers, Henry joined the ranks of Company D on October 28, 1862 and served until November 4, 1863. The Regiment was to be composed of twelve Calvary companies. Henry's service was entirely in Minnesota and he never saw any Civil War action. During the spring and summer of 1863, Henry likely participated in skirmishes with Indian war parties from the river banks of the Mississippi to those of the Missouri. In addition to fighting the Indians, the Calvary had to put up with severe drought and lack of forage for the horses. The mission complete, the various Calvary companies were disbanded during the fall and early winter of 1863. History books record the service by General Sibley and the First Regiment volunteers as being distinguished. During the short time of its existence, the Regiment lost two Officers and four Enlisted men after being

93

mortally wounded. Thirty-one additional Enlisted men were taken by disease and the lingering effects of bad weather.

Henry's military records show he served in the rank of Private for his entire time of service and it is highly unlikely that he ever was put in command of a troop. The publication "Narrative and Rosters of the Minnesota Mounted Rangers & Cavalry" also confirms this. He did eventually receive a disability pension for his service. Those records show that his pension was the result of a disability resulting from the severe cold that he experienced. It appears that he suffered from the effects of frost bite on his feet, likely incurred while in garrison during the winter of 1862-1863.

The 1865 Minnesota census indicates Henry had settled once more on his own land. Having lived as a bachelor until age 41, Henry proposed to and married Anna in 1867. With Henry's appearance and reputation, it obviously took a special woman to have him as a husband.

A year later, April 21, 1868, Anna and Henry had their first child, a girl, Annie Marie Berger. The couple go on to have seven more daughters and five sons. In order of birth, they were; John Diedrich, George Henry, Henry Herman, Maria Catherine, Joseph Gerhard, Anna Katherine, Helena, Elizabeth, Maria Francis, Francis Xavier, Maria Rosa, and Ida Marie.

After the passage of the Land Grant Act of 1862, Henry had applied for legal title to his land. He was later in filing than were his neighbors. The couple finally received the land grant title which was dated September 1, 1868. As it turns out, 1868 was momentous year for Anna and Henry.

The 1870 census was a special in that, for the first time, many more details were collected about a household and its members. It also offered a bit of humor to the Gohman family. Anna's brother, Frank, was visiting when the census enumerator came. The enumerator listed Frank as residing with Anna and Henry and being age nine. After going home, Frank was again listed as residing with his parents and being age eight. The same enumerator did both listings which were the same day and on the same census page with one neighbor family listed between them!

November 2, 1889, Henry was awarded a military disability pension for his earlier service.

Henry died February 12, 1893 of cancer and was buried February 14, 1893 in St. Mary's Help of Christians Cemetery. Obituaries were published in both the German and English language newspapers. Eight days after Henry's death, his disability pension was transferred to his widow, Anne, until she later remarried.

Anna married John Peter Lommel in 1896 but Henry's pension wasn't transferred again until January 1, 1900. It was then transferred to an Anna Lommel but one has to assume the transfer actually was to Annie Marie Berger, Henry and Anna's oldest child. Initially the family lived on the homestead of Anna's new husband in Maine Prairie, Stearns County. Between 1905 and 1910, the family moved to Manannah, Meeker County, Minnesota. John Lommel died January 30, 1912 in Eden Valley, Meeker County and was buried in Calvary Cemetery located in Eden Valley.

Anna then married Jacob Turck July 20, 1916 in Eden Valley. He died January 29, 1931 in Forest City which is also in Meeker County. Jacob was buried in St. Gertrude's Cemetery in Forest City.

Anna had died earlier on March 15, 1919 in Eden Valley. She was buried in the cemetery of her home church, St. Mary Help of Christians Cemetery, in St. Augusta on March 17, 1919.

Children of Henry and Anna (Gohman) Berger

Annie Marie (Berger) Voigt	(1868-1931)
John Diedrich Berger	(1869-1941)
George Henry Berger	(1871-1897)
Henry Herman Berger	(1873-1940)
Maria Catherine (Berger) Lubbesmeier	(1875-1923)
Joseph Gerhard Berger	(1876-1931)
Anna Katherine (Berger) Scharenbroich	(1878-1918)
Helena (Berger) Alstrom	(1880-1933)
Elizabeth (Berger) Weinand	(1882-1924)
Maria Francis (Berger) Arnold	(1884-1966)
Francis Xavier Berger	(1885-1960)
Maria Rosa (Berger) Schmit	(1887-1927)
Ida Marie (Berger) Dominik	(1889-1955)

The Berger Family

Henry Herman Berger was born November 1825 in Hanover, Lower Saxony, Germany to Herman and Elisabeth (Nũssan) Berger. His mother also went by the names Elisa or Lonnie. Apparently, Henry later became known to some of his grandchildren as Henry John Berger.

Henry, his widowed mother, and his brother, Gerhard or Georg, which he commonly used, emigrated from Germany September 1848. Departing from Bremen and declaring the men to be to be farmers, they crossed the Atlantic on the ship Post. They arrived in the United States November 10, 1848 at the port of New Orleans, Orleans, Louisiana. The Post was a sailing vessel with a barque rigging, built in 1845, and was 116 feet long. During this voyage, the Captain was George Wilhelm Haake. A typical voyage between Bremen and New Orleans for the Post was 62 days while carrying 170 passengers.

After arrival in their new homeland, Henry, his mother, and Georg traveled by steamboat up the Mississippi and Ohio rivers to Cincinnati, Hamilton County, Ohio. Henry and Georg's stay in Cincinnati is impossible to document accurately. Numerous records exist that document the residence of several Henry Bergers, Georg Bergers, Henry and Georg Berger pairs, and even trios;

several Henry, Georg and Mary Berger trios and at least one Henry, Georg and Anne Berger trio. All are of an appropriate age and the events of are appropriate timing.

Even though it is impossible to document accurately their stay in Cincinnati, it is known that the brothers lived there for some time; working as laborers. Their mother died June 1850 of cholera during an epidemic which was a raging through the immigrants at the time. During their stay in Cincinnati, Henry's brother, Georg married Mary Graussing September 27, 1853 in St. Paul's Catholic Church. Mary's maiden name is often seen spelled Gaussing. The couple had two children in Cincinnati; Mary Theresa, who apparently died shortly after birth, and Heinrich Gerhard. No records exist for Mary Theresa after her birth.

In 1856, Henry became part of a group that traveled to and settled in St. Augusta Township, Stearns County, Minnesota. Georg and family soon followed settling on a piece of property adjoining the land of his brother. Georg purchased his piece of property outright and received a land patent on July 1, 1861. During the 1900 census, his wife, Mary, reported that she had a total of nine children and six were still living. In addition to Mary Theresa and Heinrich, who were born in Cincinnati and after relocating to Minnesota; Georg and Mary gave birth to Joseph Gerhard, Anna Maria, Katherine, Magdalena, Dina Druci, Gerhard Heinich, and Susan. Records show that, in addition to Mary Theresa, at least two other children died in infancy.

Just prior to his death, Georg had an attorney draw up a will. Brother, Henry, served as a witness to the will. Georg died in December 2, 1873 and was buried in St. Mary Help of Christians Cemetery in St. Augusta. Mary remarried in 1880 to Jacob Dambly, who brought ten children to the marriage. Jacob's first wife had died in 1879. The 1890 census has Jacob and Mary living in Waite Park, Stearns County. Mary died May 5, 1905 in St. Cloud and was buried in St. Mary Help of Christians Cemetery. Jacob died February 20, 1915 and was buried in Calvary Cemetery in St. Cloud.

Henry Herman Berger (1825-1893) Family Recap

Parents:	Herman Berger	(?-1848)
	Elisabeth "Elisa or Lonnie" (Nũssan) Berger	(1772-1850)
Siblings:	George Berger	(1826-1873)
	HENRY HERMAN BERGER	(1825-1893)

Maria Elizabeth Gohmann (died as a young child)

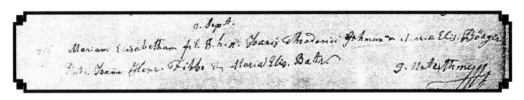

Maria Elizabeth Gohmann's baptism record excerpt

Maria Elizabeth Gohmann was born September 8, 1851 in Cincinnati, Hamilton County, Ohio. She was the third child of Diedrich and Elisabeth Gohmann. Maria Elizabeth was baptized September 9, 1851 at St. John the Baptist Catholic Church in Cincinnati. Her Godparents were John Henry Fibbe and Maria Elizabeth Batr___. (Part the name cannot be read). The presiding priest was Fr. William Unterthiner. Maria died when she was just two days short of being one year old, September 6, 1852. Her funeral was held at St. John the Baptist Catholic Church the next day and buried in the parish cemetery.

Marie Elizabeth's death was a difficult cross to bear for the growing family.

George Heinrich Gohmann and Elisabeth Theresa Witschen

George Heinrich Gohmann and Elisabeth Theresa Witchen

George Heinrich Gohmann was born July 10, 1853 in Cincinnati, Hamilton County Ohio. He was baptized the next day, July 11, 1853, at St. John the Baptist Catholic Church in Cincinnati. The baptism record made note of the fact that he was the fourth child of Diedrich and Elisabeth. His godparents were G.H.Illendorf and Maria Anna Hûlsman. The presiding priest was Edmund Etschmann. Over the years, George Heinrich became commonly known as Henry.

Just three years old, it is questionable Henry remembered much of the steamboat trip down the Ohio and up the Mississippi rivers to the new home in the Minnesota Territory. It is likely that

Henry spent some time playing with fellow traveler, Henry Toenjes, who was two years older. The youngsters must have been very popular with the older steamboat passengers.

Growing up on the homestead, Henry was expected to do homestead chores. First helping with household and garden chores and later with the crop and animals. For the next nineteen years, he helped his father, Diedrich, develop the new homestead in a new land, "grubbing" the earth for the first time to successfully harvesting the land's bounty. Henry grew to manhood learning the value of hard work and accepting whatever life brought his way.

During those same nineteen years, Henry experienced vast political change plus national and regional warfare. He learned changing farming methods and the need to adapt to changing technology.

When he was just 22 years old, April 5, 1875, Henry purchased 80 acres from his brother, Barney for $500. The land transfer document described the tract as the "South half of the Southeast quarter of Section 18 in Township 123 North, Range 27 West, containing 80 acres". A notice in the local paper April 8, 1875 also reported the sale. Immediately after the purchase, Henry began farming the land and looking for a wife.

George Heinrich Gohmann married Elisabeth Theresa Witschen November 21, 1876 in St. Augusta, Stearns County, Minnesota.

Elisabeth was born on her family's farm in St. Augusta October 28, 1856 to Johann Heinrick and Gesina Adelaide Witsken. Elisabeth had been baptized November 1, 1856 in the parent's home by Fr. Cornelius Wittmann from St. Mary Help of Christians Catholic Church. The Godparents were Charles Bernard Witschen and Anna Marie Tunnerat. The family was more commonly known as Witschen. Elisabeth was the fourth of five children; a step-brother Bernard Henry, William John, Mary Gesina, Elisabeth, and Maria Anna.

Typical of the Gohmann siblings, Henry and Elisabeth's homestead was only two miles, "as the crow flies", from the shores of the Mississippi river. At that home, they had ten children; John Diedrich, Anna Maria, Bernard Henry, John Henry, John Edward, Adelaide Theresian, Mariann Josephine, Elizabeth Dorothy, Stephen George, and Theresia Antonia. With the needs of an expanding family in mind, Henry expanded his farm by purchasing acreage from his neighbor, Henry Beumer. The deed was registered January 3, 1881.

Henry and Elisabeth suffered the double loss of a child in 1886 when twin infants, John Edward and Adelaide Theresian, died when just over four months old. The children died just twelve days apart.

Henry was remembered as "easy going" and with a quiet demeanor. Many of his children are remembered having a similar character. Henry and Elisabeth also enjoyed life and especially family gatherings. Their farm being a central location, they hosted many of the gatherings there. The barn on the property became a popular spot for barn dances. Henry and Elisabeth's grandchildren described it as the "Gohmann Hang Out". Later, a nephew or two would attempt to duplicate that warm environment by also turning their barns into "Gohmann Hang outs". Henry and Elisabeth's home also included a large porch to accommodate their many friends and family. A porch was very important to all the Gohmann siblings.

With the railroads bringing new markets for his farm production, Henry chose to support the railroad expansion. In 1882 he gave perpetual use, right of way, of a strip of land to the Minneapolis and Northwestern Railroad for the sum of $175.00.

The family of George Heinrich and Elizabeth Gohmann sitting together at their home south of St. Augusta.

Henry and Elizabeth Gohmann's Home

Henry watched, with some amazement, a changing Minnesota. In 1882, a hydroelectric power plant was built using Saint Anthony Falls to power it. It was one of the first in the United States. In 1884, iron mining began in northern Minnesota with the opening of the Soudan Mine. That opening was soon followed by others in the Vermilion and Mesabi Ranges. Large open-pit mines became common place on the Mesabi Range. These Minnesota changes created new markets and improved railroad transportation for Henry's crops.

Quite ill at the time, Henry made a will, December 31, 1903, leaving everything to his wife, Elisabeth. She was also named executor of the will. Three months later, he died on March 31, 1904 in St. Augusta, Stearns County, Minnesota of stomach cancer. He was buried April 4, 1904 in St. Mary Help of Christians Cemetery in St. Augusta.

Elisabeth died August 16, 1907 of "Bright's Disease", a kidney disease now known as acute nephritis. She was buried August 19, 1907 in St. Mary Help of Christians Cemetery. She left a will with Joseph Gohmann and William Witschen as Executors. When they declined to carry out the provisions of the will, her son, Henry, was appointed Executor by the Probate Court.

The Children of Henry and Elisabeth (Witschen) Gohman

John Diedrich Gohmann	(1878-1958)
Anna Maria (Gohmann) Beumer / Langanki	(1880-1964)
Bernard Henry Gohmann	(1882-1959)
John Henry Gohmann	(1884-1953)
John Edward Gohman	(1886-1886)
Adelaide Theresian Gohmann	(1886-1886)
Mariann Josephine (Gohmann) Potthoff	(1887-1940)
Elizabeth Dorothy (Gohmann) Frerich	(1890-1960)
Stephen George Gohmann	(1894-1918)
Theresia Antonia Gohmann	(1896-1910)

The Witschen Family

Elisabeth's father, Johann, had immigrated from Messinge, Lower Saxony, Germany to New York, United States November 19, 1850. He crossed the Atlantic on the ship Hermine. After arriving in the United States, he initially settled in Cincinnati, Hamilton County, Ohio. He most likely traveled overland to Pittsburg, Allegheny County, Pennsylvania and then by riverboat down the Ohio River to Cincinnati.

Elisabeth's mother, Gesina Adelaide Kruze, had also emigrated from Germany. She was born 1817 and may have come from somewhere in the North Rhine-Westphalia region. She emigrated from Germany, arriving in New York May 14, 1851 on the ship Carl & Emma with a man named F. Kruse and a child, B. Kruse. That child was Bernard Henry. Normally, Gesina's maiden name would have been Knochenweber. Her mother's maiden name was Kruse. Gesina's father, Johan Frances Knochenweber had taken his wife's surname of Kruse. Apparently there was a German practice of taking the wife's surname if she had inherited the family land. F. Kruse was two years younger than Gesina and could have been her husband or simply a family member. After arriving in the United States, the family settled in Cincinnati where F. Kruse seemed to have disappeared, perhaps dying. It commonly is assumed that B. Kruse was Gesina's son. A short time later, Gesina Kruse married Johann Witsken November 25, 1851 in Cincinnati's St. Joseph Catholic Church.

After the marriage Gesina's son, Bernard, assumed the Witschen name. He was born in Germany in 1849 and immigrated with his mother. Bernard died in St. Augusta July 19, 1874 and was buried in St. Mary Help of Christians Cemetery. Johann and Gesina gave birth to two other children in Cincinnati; William John and Mary Gesina, before moving to Minnesota the spring of 1856. The fall after they arrived in Minnesota, Elizabeth Theresa was born; followed by Maria Anna two years later. The family first shows up in Minnesota records during the 1857 Territorial Census.

Elisabeth's father, Johann died October 4, 1860 in St. Augusta. Her mother, Gesina, remarried to Bernard Dockmeyer. As a result of that union, Elisabeth had a new half-sister, Theresa Mary Dockmeyer.

Elisabeth's brother, William, was born in Cincinnati September 16, 1852. After the family settled in St. Augusta, Henry Krebs taught William and several other of the Witschen and Gohman children in the St. Augusta School. William married Mary Gertrude Dirks November 26, 1880 in St. Augusta. Shortly after the wedding, the couple began farming in the Clear Lake area of Sherburne County. They had eight children; Henry John, John Henry, Theodore William, Frank Anthony, Frederick Barney, Vincent Anthony, Mathilda Mary and Bernard Joseph. During 1916, William and Gertrude sold their farm and moved to St. Cloud in the Ward 4 area and lived with their son, Vincent, and his family. William died July 1933 and Mary died April 12, 1934. Both are buried in Calvary Cemetery in St Cloud.

Elisabeth's sister, Mary, was born October 26, 1854 in Cincinnati. The 1857 Minnesota census erroneously reported her place of birth as Minnesota. Mary married widower, John Ahles, November 9, 1875 and they had one child, William. John Ahles had previously been married to Elizabeth Klein and had four children. On September 17, 1879, John Ahles died leaving Elisabeth with four step children and one natural born child to raise. John had served in the Civil War with the 2nd Minnesota Regiment and was receiving a disability pension. As a widow with minor children the pension went to Mary. On June 16, 1889, the widow married Dominik Hankes in St. Wendelin Catholic Church which is located in Luxemburg, Stearns County. Dominik died November 29, 1916 and Mary died November 6, 1940 in St. Cloud.

Maria Anna Christina was Elisabeth's youngest sister. She was born September 11, 1858 and baptized 10 days later in St. Mary Help of Christians Catholic Church. She was confirmed at St. Mary's Cathedral July 2, 1871 in St. Cloud. She was commonly called Mary. Mary married John Feltes October 24, 1882 in St. Augusta. They had two children, Anna and John William. Either 1887 or 1888, John passed away. Mary then married John Goedert January 15, 1889 in St. Cloud. With John Goedert, she had five more children; Margaret, Andrew, Frank, Octavia, and Nicholas. Mary and John moved to California where she died 1920 in Los Angeles, Los Angeles County. John also died there January 3, 1937.

Elisabeth's half-sister, Theresa Mary Dockmeyer, was born July 2, 1863 in St. Augusta. She married Peter Dechene Smith November 16, 1881. The Smiths had six children; Bernard Henry, Elizabeth, John Henry, Helen Margdalen, Frances Alma, and Rose Marie. Theresa died September 22, 1930 in St. Cloud.

Elisabeth Theresa (Witschen) Gohmann (1856-1907) Family Recap

Parents:	Johann Heinrick Witsken	(1823-1860)
	Gesina Adelaide (Kruse) Witsken	(1821-1866)
Siblings:	William John Witschen	(1852-1933)
	Mary Gesina Witschen	(1854-1930)
	ELISABETH THERESA (WITSCHEN) GOHMANN	(1856-1907)
	Maria Anna Witschen	(1858-1920)
Half-siblings:	Bernard Henry Kruse/Witschen	(1849-1874)
	Theresa Mary Dockmeyer	(1863-1930)

John Diedrick Gohman and Mary Antoinette Gahr

John Diedrick Gohman and May Antoinette Gahr

John Diedrick Cantius Gohman was born October 19, 1856 in St. Augusta, Stearns County, Minnesota. His was one of the earliest recorded births in the area. John Diedrich was the fifth child in the growing Gohman family. He was baptized October 20, 1856 at the family homestead near St. Augusta, Stearns County, Minnesota. He was baptized by Fr. Cornelius Wittman, O.S.B. His godparents were John Henry Fibbe and Dina Boinie.

The first child born on the Gohman Minnesota Territory homestead, John grew to maturity on the homestead just as it was growing and developing. As he got older, John was expected to help with the homestead work. When small, helping with household and garden chores and later, when older, with the crops and animals. From his homestead experiences, he learned independence and strong personal values.

During 1873, John, his dad and brothers joined other St. Mary Help of Christians Catholic Church parishioners in building a new church. A family memory is that John felt strongly that there was a greater need for a school than a new church building. When the final decision was made to build the new church, John and Fr. Valentine Stimmler, who guided its construction, remained at odds.

From 1873 to 1878, Minnesota farmers were plagued by devastating infestations of locusts. It was eventually called "the Great Grasshopper Plague". During the same time, John's father, Diedrich and the surrounding farmers had put the majority of their land into wheat production before realizing that the locusts thrived on wheat. From those experiences, John came to understand the wisdom of farm diversification. That knowledge would guide him in later years.

During 1877 and 1878, John made trips to Northern Minnesota where he worked as a lumberjack. John was able to save some money as the pay was good and the expenses low. With his savings, John purchased the original Gohman homestead from his father, Diedrich, and step-mother, Gertrud, February 2, 1879 for $1,500.00. The bill of sale was notarized April 9, 1879. Diedrich and Gertrud continued to live on the homestead with their son.

John Gohman married Mary Antoinette Gahr January 22, 1880 in St. Paul, Ramsey County, Minnesota. Mary Antoinette was born March 14, 1861 in St. Michael, Wright County, Minnesota. She was the third child of Michael and Mary Ann (Dirks) Gahr.

In 1864, after her mother's death and her father remarried, Mary was sent to live with her Grandmother in Minneapolis. Her Uncle, Fr. Eberhart Gahr, assisted in looking after her. Mary was put to work with a local seamstress to learn the trade. Her Uncle, Fr. Gahr, played a significant role in the work of the Saint Benedictine Order in the United States. After coming from Germany, he worked out of St. Mary's Priory in Elk County, Pennsylvania, serving in Newark County, New Jersey, Kossuth County, Iowa, and various places in Minnesota, including being the first Abbot of St. John's Abbey, Collegeville. He died and was buried at St. Mary's Priory in Pennsylvania during 1922. Fr. Gahr had a reputation for getting things done and some even say that he had a hand in the marriage of Mary and John Diedrich! It would explain how a St. Augusta boy came to marry a St. Paul girl.

The 1880 census had Diedrich and Gertrude Gohman continuing to live on the original Gohman homestead with their son, John, and his new wife, Mary.

John and Mary had fifteen children; John Diedrich, Henry Herman, Anna Maria, Bernard Edward, Maria Elizabeth, Edward E., Anthony Aloysius, Francis Joseph, George, Albert Hubert, Emil Arthur, Adeline, Loretta Laura, Ida Hilda, and Mary Edella.

A family story relates that in 1893, John went to California, visiting fourteen other states as he traveled. After dealing with his wanderlust, he apparently concluded that Minnesota "was as good as anyplace".

John felt the original Gohman homestead was too small and confining. December 31, 1899, he mortgaged the homestead and purchased 300 acres of virgin forest land on the east bank of the Mississippi in Sherburne County. It was across the river and about two miles south of the original Gohman homestead in Stearns County. A predominant feature of the new land was that its western most property line fell on the eastern shore of the river where it made a large bend. The bend in the river contained several islands. The bend and its islands occasionally changed shape due to environment conditions. Each change brought about a change in the homestead's property line and arable land.

To farm any of the new land, John Diedrich first had to clear it. Knowing that it would take some time to accomplish, he rented an established farm nearby from a family named Francis. The Francis family were moving to St. Cloud, Stearns County. As that family was going to quit farming, John bought several pieces of farm equipment from them. Sometime after June 1, 1900, the family moved to the rental property for one to two years during which John cleared some of his new land and built a barn and a house.

March 25, 1902, John sold the original Gohmann homestead property to Anna T. Kiffmeyer.

The first child born on the family's new property, January 21, 1903, was John and Mary's daughter, Ida Hilda.

St. Marcus Catholic Church was established in 1888 in nearby Clear Lake, Sherburne County. John's family would naturally have gone there. At some point there was a "falling out" between John and the priest serving St. Marcus. There are several different family stories about the disagreement but no evidence to prove or disprove any of them. The issue involved may have been related to the church building and its maintenance or a request for a tithe of part of John's wheat crop. Apparently, John started attending a Methodist Church in the area while Mary attempted to keep the Catholic Faith.

John was remembered by his grandchildren as being a smart man with many skills. He was quite independent, even to the point of owning his own sawmill.

In 1908, John bought a house on what is now Killian Boulevard in East St. Cloud. Mary and some of the younger children would live there during the school year and the children would attend the St. Cloud schools. In 1910, John sold the house to his daughter, Maria Elizabeth. During the 1911 school year, Mary and the children lived with and took care of Mrs. Francis whose farm they had earlier rented. In 1912, John bought seven lots along the east shore of the Mississippi River in East Cloud and later giving right of way for what has become Riverside Drive. One lot contained an old house that was fixed up and an outbuilding added on the lot. Mary and the younger children continued to live there with John and the older children visiting every weekend bringing along firewood and supplies. This arrangement went on for a short time but then Mary and the younger children moved back to the farm and the children went to school in the Clear Lake District 9 country school.

Sometime during the summer of 1914, one of John and Mary's grandsons, Walter, wandered off. The entire family went searching for him. They even searched the river bank and shallow waters of the Mississippi. Usually the mail carrier left the family mail on the main road about a half mile from the Gohman house. That day however, the mail carrier drove his buggy around the circle in front of the house and delivered both the mail and Walter. The mail carrier had found him wandering the main road looking for "his daddy". Everyone, especially Walter's grandmother, Mary, were greatly relieved. They had pretty much made up their minds that he had drowned.

During the summer of 1917, lightning struck the Gohman home and damaged both the structure and the contents. The "Clear Lake Sherburne County Times" newspaper also reported a slight earthquake in the area.

As John and Mary's children married, some of the couples would live on the farm and help with the farm chores. On one occasion, there were four families living there. The home was a large home; four bedrooms on the second floor and one bedroom on the first floor in addition to the public rooms. The home also included a very large front porch to accommodate regular gatherings of friends and family.

John and Mary Gohman's home

The economic crash of 1929 and the "Great Depression" affected all the Gohmans. This family story is but one example how each of the Gohman families were affected.

> *"Son-in-law, Joe Klein, called John and warned him that he better get his money out of the bank because it may close. John rushed to the bank and was only allowed to withdraw $3,000 of the $10,000 that he had deposited. He was so upset that Mary, knowing he had a gun, was unsure of what he might do and took the gun and threw it into the river."*

Despite the start of the "Great Depression", January 1930, John and Mary celebrated their "Golden Anniversary". A local newspaper covered the event. The couple repeated their vows across the river at St. Mary Help of Christians Catholic Church in St. Augusta. Reverend Elmer O.S.B. was the celebrant of the High Mass. At noon, family and friends gathered at the Gohman home for dinner and an afternoon of celebration. The gathering was not as large as expected due to some unusually severe winter weather.

In addition to operating his 250 acre farm, over the years John served on the town board, the school board, and as a church trustee. John died October 3, 1934 in his bed on his homestead in Clear Lake, Sherburne County, Minnesota. John's body was "laid out" in the same room before his funeral. Despite the earlier "falling out", he was buried October 3, 1934 in Clear Lake's St. Marcus Cemetery.

Tuesday, March 14, 1944, friends and many of the Gohman ladies gathered at the Joseph Klein residence in East St. Cloud for the special occasion of Mary's 83rd birthday. As Gohmans are apt to do, the afternoon was spent playing cards and visiting. Of Mary's 15 children, 11 were still living. Thirteen of Mary's 56 grandchildren were serving in the armed forces. Her grandson, Harold

Gohman had recently died serving his country. The ladies had much to celebrate and also some serious concerns to pray about. Just three days later, Mary died March 17, 1944 in Clear Lake and was buried there in St. Marcus Cemetery. In preparation for her death, Mary had appointed Leo Gambrino as Executor of her estate.

Children of John and Mary (Gahr) Gohman

John Diedrich Gohman	(1881-1965)
Henry Herman Gohman	(1882-1964)
Anna Maria (Gohman) Noak	(1883-1903)
Bernard Edward Gohman	(1884-1912)
Maria Elizabeth [Derr] Gohman	(1886-1975)
Edward E. Gohman	(1887-1978)
Anthony Aloysius Gohman	(1889-1969)
Francis Joseph Gohman	(1889-1970)
George Gohman	(1890-1892)
Hubert Albert Gohman	(1892-1980)
Emil Arthur Gohman	(1895-1985)
Adella Gohman	(1898-1902)
Loretta Ruth (Gohman) Kerr	(1900-1991)
Ida Hilda (Gohman) Klein	(1903-1990)
Mary Adella Gohman	(1905-1906)

The Gahr Family

Mary's father, Michael was born in Pfatter, Byern, Germany in 1822 and immigrated to the United States about 1851. Michael lived for a while in Cincinnati, Hamilton County, Ohio where he met and married Mary's mother, Maria Huber, July 5, 1854. Mary's mother, Maria, was born in Germany and immigrated about the same as her future husband.

While living in Cincinnati, Mary's parents, Michael and Maria, had two boys; Michael, born March 20, 1855, and John Jacob, born September 15, 1859. Shortly after the birth of John, the family moved to St. Michael, Wright County, Minnesota. There, Mary Antoinette Gahr was born March 14, 1861.

Mary's oldest brother Michael, married Katherine Anna Becker November 3, 1886 in St. Michael, Wright County. The couple settled in Monticello, also in Wright County. They had six children; George Eberhard, Gertrude Elizabeth, Antonette Mary, Harry Albert, and Theron Cusmus. Katherine died July 20, 1902. Sometime after the 1920 census, the family moved to Olmstead County, Minnesota. Michael died there April 7, 1944. Both Michael and Katherine were buried in St. Michael's Cemetery in St. Michael.

The middle child, John Jacob, married Margaret M. Bodems September 1863. They had eight children; Lena C., Michael Edward, Florence J., Alma E., Alfred John, Mathilda M., Louis L., and Herbert J. The family lived in St. Cloud until sometime between 1900 and 1916 when they moved to Siglunes, Manitoba, Canada. John died there June 5, 1934.

Shortly after Mary's birth, her mother died May 2, 1861 in St. Michael and was buried in St. Michael Cemetery. July 5th of that same year, Mary's dad, Michael, married Maria Burges. They had one son, Joseph, who was born June 30, 1863. Michael registered for the Civil War draft that July. Three months later, October 25, 1863, he was killed in a hunting accident in Stearns County. Maria Burges then remarried to Hubertus Barthel on January 15, 1864. She died February 14, 1929 in St. Michael.

Mary Antoinette (Gahr) Gohman (1861-1944) Family Recap

Parents:	Michael Gahr	(1822-1863)
	Mary Ann (Dirks) Gahr	(?-1861)
Siblings:	Michael N. Gahr	(1855-1944)
	John Jacob Gahr	(1859-1934)
	MARY ANTOINETTE (GAHR) GOHMAN	(1861-1944)
Half-sibling:	Joseph Gahr	(1863-?)

Joseph Gohmann and Rosa Maria Koenig

Joseph Gohman and Rosa Maria Koenig

Joseph Gohmann was born May 31, 1859 in St. Augusta, Stearns County, Minnesota.

The second child born on the Gohman Minnesota Territory homestead, Joseph grew to maturity there. As he grew up, Joseph helped with home and farm chores which became physically more demanding as he grew older and stronger. When small, helping with household and garden chores and later, when older, with the crops and animals. From his homestead experiences, he learned independence and strong personal values.

111

As early as 1856, there were plans for a bridge to cross the Mississippi in St. Cloud. It was to be located at the site of the St. Germain ferry landing. By 1868, the bridge existed in the form of a crude toll bridge. At some point, a decision was made to make it a public bridge. The bridge was allowed to deteriorate and was eventually taken down. About 1880, a replacement bridge was under construction. In 1884, the new substantial St. Germain Bridge was put in service. The new Mississippi crossing made practical the expansion of the Gohman family across the river. Although his brother, John Diedrick, had already settled in Sherburne County, Joseph understood what this new opportunity would bring and was the next Gohman to take advantage of it.

The 1885 Sherburne County Census has Joseph, age 26, living by himself and incorrectly listing his place of birth as being Germany. He was homesteading 120 acres by himself. He had originally settled on the land as early as 1880. A bachelor living on a large established homestead, Joseph found himself looking for a wife.

No records could be found to confirm the amazing and amusing family story about the events leading up to Joseph and Rosa Marie Koenig's marriage. The story goes something like this:

> *"Joseph homesteaded some land three miles north east of Clear Lake, Sherburne County. That was in 1880 when he was 21 years old. He lived alone there in a two room house for eight years. Joseph met neighbor Joseph Koenig and found out he had a sister named Rose about his age. Joseph promised Joseph Koenig a pair of good buckskin gloves, if he would arrange a meeting between them. The two men cooked up a plan. When Joseph Gohmann went to see Joseph Koenig, he went into the house to ask his sister, Rose, to open the gate for Joseph Gohmann who was waiting down the road. In this way they met and talked about getting married. Just before the marriage, Joseph took Rose to his sister's house in St. Cloud and she made a wedding dress for Rose. On January 11, 1887 they were married in St. Augusta Catholic Church. He then took her home to his farm and she cooked a wedding supper of side pork and potatoes."*

The Gohman story might be wrong in one regard. The couple's marriage license indicates that Joseph Gohmann married Rosa Maria Koenig January 11, 1887 in St. Cloud, Benton County, Minnesota. The presiding priest was Fr. F.X.A. Stemper who was the parish priest for Holy Angels Catholic Church. In addition, he was vicar general of the Apostolic Vicariate of Northern Minnesota which became the Diocese of St Cloud two years later. Although, the couple's marriage license was in Benton County, they married in St. Cloud; most likely at Holy Angels Catholic Church. Father F.X.A. Stemper performed the ceremony with Stephen Gohman and Elizabeth Koenig as witnesses. Fr. Stemper went on to be a missionary in Puerto Rico in 1853. In 1885, he served Lake Catholic Church, Belgium, Ozauke, Wisconsin. He also served as a chaplain in the Spanish-American war of 1898. In 1915, he was the first priest at Holy Family Catholic Church in Spokane, Washington.

Rosa Maria was born February 24, 1863 in St. Rosa, Mercer County, Ohio to Erhard Johannes Koenig and Mary Ann Dirks.

Joseph and Rosa had seven children; John Joseph, Mary Elizabeth, August Henry, Rose Ann, Cyril Anton, Emma Elizabeth, and Christine Mary. They lost their son, Cyril, when he was only four years and 3 months old when he died from diphtheria. Future generations often commented on how attractive Rosa and the children were, especially August. With his marriage, Joseph started a journal in the family bible of family births, marriages, and deaths.

Joseph purchased a listing in the 1914 Sherburne Farmers Directory. It indicated that he owned 160 acres in Section 10 and 80 acres in Section 9 of Clear Lake Township. The family members listed were Joseph, Rose, John, Rose, Emma, and Christine. The listing indicated that they had resided in the county for 32 years and were served by the Clear Lake post office. The 1914 Sherburne County Platt book only had Joseph owning the land in Section 10 while the 1916 edition indicated his ownership of the land in both sections. From that, it is obvious that Joseph had just recently purchased 80 acres in Section 9 from D. Woodbury. The seller was likely a descendant or sibling of Caleb Woodbury, a citizen of Michigan, who possessed a large number of land claims in Sherburne County, Minnesota. The 1914 edition also listed the landowner as "Jno Gohman" vice "Jos Gohman". The 1916 edition also corrected his name. It is highly likely that funds from the sale of the 80 acres originally acquired from the Elizabeth Gohman estate made this latest purchase possible.

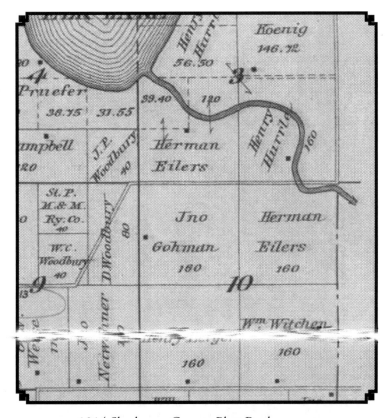

1914 Sherburne County Platt Book excerpt

Joseph and Mary's son, August Henry, returned home from Kansas City, Kansas March 28, 1918, where he had been working on the automotive industry. He was seriously ill when he arrived. Mary nursed her son, August, for about two weeks before he died. Mary wrote a sorrowful Mother's letter to her daughter, Mary Elizabeth, telling her about the passing of her brother.

1934 was a big year for Joseph and Rosa with a trip to Strome, Alberta, Canada to visit their daughter Mary Elizabeth. After their daughter's marriage to John Machtemes, the couple had begun homesteading just outside Strome. Joseph and Rosa especially enjoyed seeing ten of their grandchildren. Rosa often wrote to her daughter, Mary Elizabeth, but a personal visit was a special treat.

Sometime in 1921, Rosa was hit by a street car and suffered internal injuries. When she died 2:40PM Sunday February 10, 1935 in Clear Lake, that incident and injuries were listed on her death certificate as contributing to the cause of death. She had been sick for about two months and primary cause of death was cancer. Rosa was buried February 13, 1935 in St. Marcus Cemetery, also in Clear Lake. Fr. Zitur officiated at the funeral service. Of her five surviving children; John, Emma, and Christine were able to attend and comfort their father, Joseph.

During 1937, Joseph, again, visited his daughter, Mary Elizabeth in Canada. Mary and her husband were considering a move to a new homestead near Fort Assiniboine, Alberta, Canada. Joseph made the trip with his daughters Emma and Christine and their spouses.

Joseph died February 26, 1946 in Clear Lake, Sherburne County, Minnesota. The cause of death was given as senility but he had been suffering from hypertension for three years and arterial sclerosis for five years. Joseph was buried February 28, 1946 in St. Marcus Cemetery.

Children of Joseph and Rosa (Koenig) Gohmann

John Joseph Gohmann	(1888-1940)
Mary Elizabeth (Gohmann) Machtemes	(1889-1960)
August Henry Gohmann	(1892-1918)
Rose Anna (Gohman) Appel	(1894-1974)
Cyril Anton (Gohmann)	(1897-1901)
Emma Elizabeth (Gohmann) Etnier	(1900-1970)
Christine Mary (Gohmann) Staneart	(1903-1981)

The Koenig Family

Rosa's father, Erhard or John as he was commonly called, emigrated from Germany with his parents and three siblings between 1830 and 1837. During their relocation, the spelling of their name changed from König in Germany to Koenig in the United States. As happened to many who were emigrating it most likely occurred as the result of a misspelled listing on the ship's manifest.

The family settled in Mercer County, Ohio in an area known as St. Rosa which was being settled by pious Catholics. To this day the area is known for its Catholic Churches; each with a cross atop their respective spires. Their homestead was also near what has become the Shrine of the Holy Relics in Maria Stein, Ohio.

Rosa, her parents, and siblings moved to Minnesota in 1872. At the time, her siblings included; Joseph, Frank, Bernard, Alois who was also known as Morris, and Elisabeth. Her siblings, Henry John and Annie, were born in St. Augusta, Stearns County. The 1880 census had the entire family living in St. Augusta. Just after the 1880 census, Rosa's sister, Mary, was born. In 1881, the family moved to a Haven Township homestead in nearby Sherburne County.

With the exception of Rosa, the entire family remained intact on the home place until, at least, the 1895 census. After Rosa's father, John, passed away August 24, 1900, her mother, Mary, brother, Joseph, and sister, Mary, moved to St. Cloud, Stearns County. The 1905 census had them living on 13th avenue north.

Rosa's brother, Joseph, was born 1863 in Ohio; most likely in St. Rosa. Until his father's death, Joseph had farmed with him. When Joseph, his mother, and sister moved to St. Cloud, Joseph became a stone cutter. By 1920, Joseph had moved the two ladies and himself to Bowman, Bowman County, North Dakota and had taken up farming. Two other Central Minnesota families had also relocated to the area; the Henry Koenig and George Fibbe families. All three family groups lived near each other. Rosa's mother died in Bowman November 23, 1923. Joseph and Mary continued to live there and appear in the 1925 state census. Siblings, Joseph and Mary, both remained unmarried. No records about them can be found after 1925. Some family historians' report Joseph died April 17, 1930 in Sherburne County but that has never been confirmed.

Frank was born 1866 in Ohio; again most likely in St. Rosa. Between 1895 and 1902, he married Katherine Velah. Frank and his wife began farming in Clear Lake Township, Sherburne County. They had four boys; George, Joseph, Leo, and Anthony. By the time of the 1905 census, Frank and his family were again using the German spelling of their family name, König. Later documents showed the use of both name variations. By 1930, Frank and family moved to St. Augusta Township. Frank, Katherine and two of the boys were renting a farm. He died there May 16, 1940. He was buried in St. Mary Help of Christians Cemetery.

Bernard was born June 5, 1868 in Marion, Mercer County, Ohio. In 1897, he married Anna Maria Hinkemaier October 1891 in Stearns County. They initially lived in St Cloud where Bernard became a granite polisher. Bernard and his wife are known to have had two children; John and Mary. Sometime before 1940, Bernard and his wife, Anna, moved and rented a place in Minneapolis, Hennepin County. Bernard did a variety of work while living there, including painting and general laborer. Bernard died March 27, 1945 and Anna died January 30, 1956. Both were buried in St. Anthony Cemetery.

Alois, listed as Morris on at least one census, was born June 21, 1870 in Mercer County, Ohio; most likely in Marion. After the 1895 census in Haven, Sherburne County, he moved to St. Paul, Ramsey County. Alois died there January 21, 1918.

Rosa's sister, Elisabeth, was born October 1, 1872 somewhere in Ohio; most likely in Marion. She married Wallace V. Davee May 1, 1889 in Sherburne County. Wallace had relocated from Maine. They had, at least, thee children; William J., Arthur W., and Caroline. Elisabeth died December 26, 1918 in Clear Lake and was buried in Clear Lake Cemetery. Wallace died November 22, 1929 Dover-Foxcroft, Piscataquis, Maine.

Henry John was born September 28, 1874 in St Augusta. Henry, first married Christiana Roering November 5, 1900 and then Lauretta Heinen July 6, 1916 in Bowman North Dakota. By 1910, Henry and Christina had moved to Bowman, North Dakota and had three children; Joseph, Mary Leonelle, and Christine Marie. Between 1910 and 1916, Christina died. Henry died July 1, 1953 in Beresford, Union County, South Dakota. Henry's second wife was originally from New Ulm, Brown County, Minnesota and both were buried in New Ulm Catholic Cemetery.

Annie was born 1878 in St. Augusta.

Rosa's youngest sister, Mary Gertrude, was born September 1880 in St. Augusta. After her father's death, Mary moved with her mother to St. Cloud and then to Bowman, North Dakota.

Rosa Maria (Koenig) Gohman (1863-1935) Family Recap

Parents:	Erhard Johannes Koenig	(1837-1900)
	Mary Ann (Dirks) Koenig	(1840-1923)
Siblings:	ROSA MARIA (KOENIG) GOHMAN	(1863-1935)
	Joseph Koenig	(1864-1930)
	Frank Koenig	(1866-1940)
	Bernard Koenig	(1868-1945)
	Alois "Morris" Koenig	(1870-1918)
	Elisabeth (Koenig) Davee	(1872-1918)
	Henry John Koenig	(1874-1953)
	Annie Koenig	(1878-?)
	Mary Koenig	(1880-?)

Frank Jerome Gohmann (died as a teen)

Frank Jerome Gohmann was born in St. Augusta, Stearns County, Minnesota September 23, 1861. He was baptized September 30, 1861 at St. Mary Help of Christians Catholic Church in St. Augusta. His Godparents were Francis Michael Hurle and Katherine Volsberg.

Frank was listed twice in the 1870 census. He was first listed as age 9 and residing with his sister, Annie, and Her husband, Henry. Then he was listed as age 8 and residing with his parents. Both listings were by the same census enumerator, the same day and on the same census page with one neighbor family listed between them!

Frank died October 1874 and was buried in St. Mary Help of Christians Cemetery in St. Augusta.

Frank Jerome Gohmann's tombstone

Anna Maria Elizabeth Gohmann and Angelo Gambrino

Anna Maria Elizabeth Gohmann and Angelo Gambrino

Anna Maria Gohmann was born July, 7, 1864 in St. Augusta, Stearns County, Minnesota. She was the eighth child of Diedrich and Elisabeth Gohmann. She was mostly likely baptized at St. Mary Help of Christians Catholic Church. However, no birth or baptism records for her have been found.

The youngest of three daughters, Anna was still expected to "hold her own" by helping with the household chores. The first twenty years of her life brought major highly publicized changes to the lives of women in the United States. They included several independent women becoming nationally famous, women's magazines becoming popular, creation of the first all-woman state college, and the beginning of the suffrage movement. Despite these external influences, Anna learned from her mother and sisters how to best support and encourage the men of the household as they pursued their careers. Anna was often called "Lizzie" by those that knew her.

At twenty years old, Anna Maria Elizabeth Gohmann married Anton Gambrino February 5, 1884 at St. Mary Help of Christians Catholic Church in St. Augusta. The witnesses were Joseph Gohman and Marie Hall. The marriage registry included the names of Angelo's parents; Anton Giamberini and Rosa Bossie.

Angelo Giamberini was born April 18, 1854 in, what is now, Azzate, Varese, Lombardia, Italy. It was also the hometown of his father, Anton Giamberini, and his mother, Rosa Bossi, came from nearby, Milan. After his immigration to the United States, Angelo chose a new name, Anton Gambrino.

After their marriage, Anna and Anton settled into a home on 16th avenue south in St. Cloud. The 1894 St. Cloud City Directory lists Anton and his family living in house number 27 on that avenue. By 1905, the family had moved to 1st Street and 11th avenue north. Later that house was taken off its foundation and moved to a different lot. Anton built a new home for the family on the original lot but with a new address, 1014 1st street north. The 1905 St. Cloud census document listed Anton and his family as in Ward 2.

Anna and Anton had two children, Anna and Leo Bernard. Their daughter, Anna, died when she was just short of five years old.

Anton was a carpenter by trade and helped build many structures in the Stearns County area, including several churches. A picture exists of Anton working on the steeple of St. Alexius Catholic Church in West Union. He also helped build the Catholic Church in Clear Lake, Sherburne County. A Gambrino family story relates that Anton and Anna lived in Clear Lake while the church was being built from 1888 to 1889. Anton's sphere of influence went well beyond the carpenter trade. He was well known and respected by many of the community business men and leaders.

February 6, 1918, Anton began the steps to become a United States citizen. It is interesting that his Declaration of Intent carries the letter head of the Department of Labor, Naturalization Service. Immigration and naturalization in the United States was all about growing the county's skilled labor pool.

In addition to her household chores and supporting Anton in his endeavors, Anna was very active in her church. Those activities included St. Ann's, St. Margaret's and the Rosary societies plus she was a member of the Third Order of St. Francis. At some point Anna created, in German, a list of important family events. It is likely that she took some of the information from a bible belonging to the family Matriarch and Patriarch.

Anna Gambrino

Anton retired from carpentry during 1924. Despite the earlier hard physical effort of being a carpenter, Anton suffered from heart and circulatory problems during his six year retirement. He was under a doctor's care beginning December 1, 1929 for those ailments. Anton died 11:30, March 6, 1930 in his St. Cloud home. He was in his bedroom when he collapsed and died. As was common then, Anton was laid out in a casket in the living room of the house and the family received the many well-wishers there. After a funeral mass at St. Mary's Catholic Church, Anton was buried in Calvary Cemetery, St. Cloud on March 8, 1930. The list of pall-bearers, honorary and actual, was a testament of the level of respect that Anton had achieved in his new homeland.

On a Thursday night, January 8, 1931, Anna died in St. Cloud at the home of her son, Leo, of bronchial pneumonia and asthma. She had experienced trouble breathing for about two years. Like her husband, Anna was laid out in a casket in her son's home for the four days leading up to her burial at Calvary Cemetery in St. Cloud.

Children of Anton and Anna (Gohmann) Gambrino

Anna Gambrino	(1891-1896)
Leo Bernard Gambrino	(1895-1969)

The Gambrino Family

After Angelo's father died, his mother remarried. As a result of the marriage, Angelo acquired an older step brother with whom a positive sibling relationship was impossible. Frustrated by the family relationship, in 1879, when Angelo was 25, he left his mother and home in Italy, crossed the Alps and traveled to Germany.

A story passed down through the family is that Angelo worked in quarries throughout Europe. The story also indicates Angelo could not read or write and was unable to communicate with his mother as he traveled. This is most likely true as his naturalization intent document was signed with an "X" and it was indicated as his "mark" because he could not sign his name. Another family story has Angelo traveling to what is known as the Ruhr district of Germany to work in the coal mines. This is quite likely the course Angelo followed as that region's industry was booming and the demand for coal as fuel was intense. The local coal mines, known as colliers, were recruiting employees from far and wide. While most of the recruits were from the Polish speaking areas of Europe, young men from the northern Italian peninsula were also heeding the call. Up until 1859, the area where Angelo was born had been governed by Austrian rulers with strong German influence. Those rulers governed an area that was known as Bohemia which included parts of modern day Austria, Hungary, and Czechoslovakia. While the northern Italian peninsula was semi-independent and not part of Bohemia, the Austrian ruling ties made it seem so. That early life exposure to the Germanic influence could have contributed to Angelo being drawn to the opportunities in the Ruhr region.

Living in Europe during that time had to be an exciting experience for a young man. There was constant and ongoing political intrigue and periodic pockets of revolutionary insurrection. Angelo was a firsthand witness to the initial events leading up to World War I. In 1882, after three years in Germany, the 28 year old Angelo left Europe and immigrated to the United States. Angelo was on the leading edge of what would become a historic level of emigration from Italy to the United States.

Angelo departed through the port of Bremen, Germany, made a stopover in Southampton, England, and proceeded to New York. His passage was on the ship Neckar and he arrived in New York on May 15, 1882. He was Neckar passenger 604 on the New York Passenger Arrival Registry for that date and ship. He was listed by his given name, Angelo Giamberini and his place of origin is listed as Bohemia. As a new immigrant in a new land, after his arrival, Angelo chose a new name, Anton Gambrino.

Anton made friends with a son of another immigrant family on the ship, Matthew Hall. The Hall family had prearranged plans to settle in St. Cloud, Stearns County, Minnesota. Apparently, Anton felt that if St. Cloud was good enough for his new friend's family, it was good enough for him. After arriving in New York, he made his way across the Eastern United States to St. Cloud. It is likely he traveled from New York to the St. Cloud area by train. Various railroad companies had been established with connections linking New York with Central Minnesota. Anton would have traveled during a period when smaller railroads were merging into vast transportation empires with wealthy and powerful railroad barons. During 1882, there were several "Orphan Trains" from New York to Central Minnesota. Maybe, Anton had the unique experience of traveling with the orphans who were also looking for new homes. While living in Europe, Anton had become proficient in the German language which was invaluable when he arrived in St. Cloud. Many German immigrants had settled in Stearns County and the language was commonly used in everyday business and even during Catholic Masses.

Anton Gambrino (1854-1930) Family Recap

Parents:	Anton Giamberini	(?-?)
	Rosa Bossi	(?-?)
Siblings:	ANTON GAMBRINO	(1854-1930)

Stephen Gohman and Catherine Wamka

Stephen Gohman was born February 1, 1867 in St. Augusta, Stearns County, Minnesota. He was baptized by Fr. Antonius, O.S.B. February 3, 1867 at St. Mary Help of Christians Catholic Church. His godparents were Stephan Hinkemeier and Maria Elisabeth Moeller.

The "baby" of the Gohman family, Stephen was still expected to hold his own while doing the chores that farming demanded. As his other siblings married and left the homestead, he helped his brother, John, by shouldering an increasing share of the homestead work. This encouraged Stephen to striking out on his own at a very young age.

Following the lead of his older brother, Joseph, Stephen began looking for land across the Mississippi in Sherburne County. His land search led him to property in Sherburne County about a mile from his brother's farm.

By age 22, Stephen Gohman owned 156 acres, more or less. The property was described as "North West one quarter, Section Eleven, Township Thirty Four, Range Twenty-nine, excepting the northwest 4 acres". He bought the land from Alanson C. Potter with wife Mary H. Potter and Charles W. Potter with wife Clara B. Potter January 17, 1889 for $1000.00.

Stephen "Steve" Gohman married Catherine Wamka June 30, 1890 in Benton County, Minnesota. The marriage license document has her listed as Warhke. The marriage was conducted by a Catholic Priest, E. J. Murphy with witnesses D. Berger and Theres Walters. Although no marriage record has been found, it is safe to assume that the marriage took place at Sts. Peter and Paul Catholic Church in what is now Gilman, Benton County, Minnesota.

It is quite likely that Catherine was born July 1867 in or near Gadebusch a town in western part of an area historically known as Pomerania. That historic area includes parts of what is now modern day Eastern Germany and Western Poland. Her parents were Johann and Hedwig Wienke. It is uncertain what Hedwig's maiden name was but it may have been Möller. Catherine was more commonly called "Katie".

Stephen and Catherine had three children; Teresiann Anna, Frederick Henry and Paul Joseph.

Catherine Gohman and children

No verifiable picture of Stephen is known to exist. Both of Stephen's sons were described as medium build and height with blue eyes and dark brown hair. It is likely that they inherited their appearance from their father.

Stephen Gohman died September 25, 1895 in Clear Lake, Sherburne County, Minnesota and was buried there September 28, 1895 in St. Marcus Cemetery. A transcription taken from St Marcus Cemetery records includes a statement by an area Elder. He stated:

> *"Stephen owned their farm-had wife-2 children. They were thrashing grain stacks and stopped to eat dinner. Stephen died in his Father's/Fred arms at dinner table. His dad Fred bought the farm from his widow."*

The following Thursday, the Der Nordstern, a local paper published in German, ran his obituary. It translates as:

> *"Last Wednesday afternoon, a very sad accident befell the family of Stephan Gohmann of Clear Lake. Suddenly they lost the father of the family. Mr. Gohmann was working with a Thrashing machine crew, and while they were at lunch, he suddenly fell backwards to the ground and died. A heart attack took his life. The funeral was on Saturday. He leaves to mourn him his wife and two small children. Our sympathy to these and eternal rest to the deceased."*

Stephen Gohman's tombstone

Catherine "Katie" Gohman, widow, sold the farm land to Herman Eilers and wife Terasia Eilers June 5, 1896 for $1,200.

After Catherine's husband, Steve Gohman, died in 1895, she married George Martin November 26, 1896 in Benton County. The marriage was conducted by Reverend John Belzowski with witnesses Louis and Rosy Templin. Catherine and George had three children, Thomas, Marie, and Sylvester John. The 1900 census listed their household in Granite Ledge, Benton County. Sometime between 1907 and 1920, Catherine and George divorced. The 1920 census has her living in St. Cloud along with three of her children; Paul Gohman, Marie Martin, and Sylvester John Martin. George Martin died April 23, 1927 in Itasca County.

The 1930 census lists Catherine living with her son, Sylvester Martin and wife, Cora, in Minneapolis, Hennepin County. The obituary of Catherine's son, Frederick Gohman, indicated she was still living in Minneapolis in 1935. Catherine died there March 11, 1943 and was buried in St. Anthony's Cemetery in Minneapolis.

The children of Stephen and Catherine (Wamka) Gohman

Teresiann Anna (Gohman) Hill	(1892-1949)
Frederick Henry Gohman	(1884-1935)
Paul Joseph Gohman	(1895-1951)

The Wamka Family

The Wamka family actions indicated that they were of Polish descent but some documents indicate they came from Germany. The region the family came from was initially inhabited by Slavic tribes that included the Polan and Kashubian peoples. Prior to the time of the generations of this story, the area was fought over and portions ruled by many political entities including the Holy Roman Empire, Sweden, and various Germanic governments including Prussia. Starting around 1806 Prussia, France, Sweden, and Denmark raged wars for portions or all of the Pomerania area. Despite the influence of the warring parties, members of the early Slavic tribes remained fiercely independent and maintained a strong allegiance to a Polish heritage with strong ties to the Catholic Church. At the time, there existed in Pomerania a very large population of Wienke's and they all considered themselves part of the Polish heritage groups.

Since the middle ages, Pomerania Catholics had been assigned to the Polish Diocese of Leslau and Polish was the church language. Even after Lutheranism and the Protestant Reformation had reached the area, the descendants of the early Slavic tribes remained Roman Catholic. In power in 1843, the Prussian parliament changed the official church language from Polish to German but the Pomeranian Catholic Churches were quickly reverted to Polish.

As 1870 approached, Prussia and its influence was expanding rapidly. The Catholic Poles found themselves segregated into their own world, living in the country or restricted city neighborhoods. They sent their children to separate public schools where the Catholic Faith was taught. There was little integration and the Protestants were a higher social status while Catholics were likely to be tenant farmers or unskilled workers. The initial phases of what became known as Kulturkampf, which was officially launched in 1872, were being felt. The government was taking charge of religious and educational affairs through the funding of the schools, including the Catholic schools. In planning was the abolishment of the Catholic section of the Prussian Ministry of ecclesiastical and educational affairs. Catholics would then lose their voice in their own affairs. The new system would be anti-Polish and anti-Catholic and would target the area where the Wienkes lived. Because of the worsening conditions, many "Polish Catholic" families, including a large number of Wienke families, began immigrating to America.

In their various documents, Catherine's family primarily used Poland as their home of origination with some listing Germany. Those uses are reflected in the text of this book.

An understanding of the family story would be impossible without some clarification about their use of names. Like the Gohmans, this family, as did most other Weinke families, used several variants of their surname to include; Weincke, Warhke, Wamke, and Wamka. Generally, they went by Weinke before emigration from Europe and Wamka after immigration to the United States. However, family related documents show they were not consistent in doing so.

In the European region the family came from, it was common to baptize children and give them numerous names. Four given names was the norm and even six names was not unusual. Amongst the Weinke's of the region, a female baby was normally given some combination of traditional Polish names; Catherina, Sophia, Dorothea, Hedwig, Jadwiga, Elisabeth, Marianne, Mina, and derivatives of these and others. The male babies were given a combination of Johann, Joachim, Frederick, Heinrich, Hans, and also derivatives of these and others. As the children grew up, they often varied which of their given names they used in everyday life.

Catherine's Mother usually went by the name Hedwig which was a German derivative of a favored Polish women's name that originated with a famous early Polish King during the Polish-Lithuanian Alliance. That King was a woman but was crowned as a King rather than a Queen. The story even gets stranger as Hedwig also used the Polish derivative of the name, Jadwiga. Catherina's father simply used the name John. Catherina Margaret chose to be called Catherine or simply "Kate" for most purposes.

To add to the confusion, Catherine indicated in various documents that her birth year was 1867, 1870, 1871, 1872, and 1873. Also, sometimes she gave her place of birth as Chicago, Illinois, sometimes as Poland, and sometimes as Germany. Another confusing set of issues when researching Catherine's family include families with similar names and dates living in the same areas; especially Gadebusch, Germany; Chicago, Cook County, Illinois and Alberta Township, Benton County, Minnesota. There also was a family with similar names and dates living in St. Paul, Ramsey County, Minnesota. Also an issue for anyone studying the family was the strange fact that when listing the family in census records it appears that only the oldest child still at home was listed. There are a few other examples of families doing this but the reason for it is unknown.

Catherine, her mother, and three sisters; Marianne, Johanna, and Anna, emigrated June 20, 1873 through the port of Hamburg, Germany. The women of the family's passage to New York, New York, United States was via Liverpool, England on the ship "Hansa". Catherine's father, John, preceded them December 19, 1871. His passage to New York from Hamburg was on the ship "Cumberland" which also made a stopover in Liverpool, England.

Catherine's father, John, had settled in Chicago, Cook County, Illinois. On his emigration documents, John gave his occupation as a laborer. At the time, Chicago was a booming industrial town and German, Polish, and other European laborers were being recruited to those industries. John easily found work there and established himself in a community of people with a similar background. It is not certain how the family made its way from New York to Chicago. They may have traveled overland by train or by ship via the Great Lakes. Chicago had recently become a major railroad hub and train is the most likely way they traveled.

The great Chicago fire occurred in 1871 and the family arrived during the huge rebuilding effort. Chicago's Polish immigrants settled in clusters known as "Polish Patches". Because of Catherine's mother's name, Hedwig / Jadwiga, perhaps they settled in a "Polish Patch" known as "Jadwigowo". It was an area around St. Hedwig's Catholic Church. Another daughter, Rosa, was born in their new home.

An area in the Gilmanton Township, Benton County, Minnesota, part of which became Alberta Township and near the current Village of Gilman was attracting Polish immigrants who rented or purchased small homesteads that existed there. The area was called "Alberta Colony" by several prominent Polish businessmen in Chicago who promoted it. After 1877, the area began growing rapidly. After hearing of this opportunity and because of their Polish roots, the family was drawn to and settled there sometime between 1877 and 1880. The first record of their presence was the 1880 census which listed Catherine's father, John, as a farmer. Her father, John died January 17, 1917 in St. Cloud, Stearns County.

Although having a name not usually associated with a Polish heritage, the Polish immigrant Martin family lived nearby. Later, widower Catherine would marry one of their children.

There is some uncertainty about information concerning Catherine's oldest sister. It is thought that Marianne was born 1858 in Poland. It is also thought that while the family lived in Chicago, Marianne married Joseph Mitchell and began using the name Mary. If that is the case, sometime before 1881, Joseph and Mary moved to Minnesota where they had a daughter, Kate. By 1939, the Mitchell family had returned to Chicago where Mary died March 4, 1942 and was buried in Evergreen Park Cemetery on March 7th.

Catherine's youngest living sister, Rosa, was born January 1876 in Chicago. She married Anthony Templin May 28, 1895 in Benton County. Anthony had been born August 18, 1863 in Poland and he, his parents, and eight siblings also lived in Chicago from 1873 to sometime before the 1885 Alberta Township census. They farmed property near the Martin family named earlier. After marrying, Anthony and Rosa owned a small farm also in Alberta Township. They were known to have had two daughters; Freda or Anne and Katherine. Anthony died November 10, 1923 in Gilman, Benton County and was buried there in St. Peter and Paul's Catholic Church Cemetery. Their daughter Freda had gone to work in St. Paul, Ramsey County and almost immediately after Anthony's death, Rosa and the other daughter, Katherine, also moved to St. Paul. All three women lived together and worked as cleaning ladies in two of St. Paul's hospitals.

Catherine's mother had seven children with six surviving in 1900. That means Catherine had 4 other siblings that little is known about; possibly a son, Jochen, born around 1861, Jenna born 1863, Johanna born 1867, and Anna born 1869. All were born in Germany.

Catherine (Wamka) Gohman (1867-1943) Family Recap

Parents:	Johann Wienke	(1836-1917)
	Hedwig??	(1834-?)
Siblings:	Marianne (Wamka) Mitchell	(1858-1942)
	Jochen Hans Heinrich Wienke	(1861-?)
	Jennie/Jenna Wamka	(1863-?)
	Johanna Wienke	(1867-?)
	CATHERINE (WAMKA) GOHMAN	(1867-1943)
	Anna Wienke	(1870-?)
	Rosa (Wamka) Templin	(1876-?)

Church, Village and Neighbors

Early Church and Village

Although members of the Gohman family have spread out across the entire country, St. Mary Help of Christians Catholic Church and the Village of St. Augusta remain the family's home church and town. The early history of the family overlaps that of both the village and the church.

The original Village of St. Augusta plat was laid out along the Mississippi River just north of what became the Diedrich Gohmann homestead. Fr. Francis X. Pierz established a mission in the new village that would become St. Mary Help of Christians Catholic Church. Although each have earlier events leading up to it, 1856 is accepted as the establishment of the homestead, village, and church. There is one early story that relates that Fr. Pierz found a picture of St. Augustine during one of his earliest visits and suggested the name "St. Augustine" be used for the new community.

Just as the Gohmann homestead initially struggled but then flourished, so did the Village of St. Augusta. Starting with a simple lumber mill, it quickly added two general stores, a blacksmith shop, wagon factory, and even two doctor's offices. A Postmaster was even appointed and the town's first post office established. A tornado destroyed the village in 1859 and it was never fully rebuilt. About a mile south of the current St. Augusta, a new town had been platted. That town was to be called Neehah City. Although a flour mill was built there, no other development took place.

Although the survival of the Village of St. Augusta was temporarily in doubt, the church continued to flourish. The small log church that Fr. Pierze had built in 1856 quickly became too small and a wood frame church was constructed. Outgrowing the church a second time, in 1872 the parish began looking at new locations. In 1873, it was decided to build a new St. Mary Help of Christians Catholic Church at a new location. Property about a mile west of the original Village of St. Augusta site was acquired. Parishioners including Diedrich and his sons worked together to build the new church under the leadership of the parish priest, Fr. Valentine Stimmler. Later, but part of the church relocation, remains in the original church cemetery were exhumed and moved to a new cemetery adjacent to the new church building. The family Matriarch was among those relocated. During the years since, many Gohman descendants were buried in the St. Mary Help of Christians Cemetery.

Soon businesses followed and located near and around the new church. The first general store was opened by Henry Beumer. It was followed in two years by a second general store operated by John Mayer. The stores included stables where church goers could leave their horses while attending church or doing business in town. A blacksmith shop, a produce storage building, and other businesses followed. Utilizing a horse drawn wagon, one of the St. Augusta businesses began home delivery of milk to the residents of nearby St. Cloud. With the arrival of regular train service, a train depot was built in St. Augusta. Even to this day, St. Augusta sometimes struggles with its own identity but St. Mary Help of Christians Catholic Church remains its strength.

Neighbors

Clustered around the Gohmann homestead were the homesteads of families who were long time acquaintances. Many of the neighbors had also come from the Ankum and Damme areas of Germany via time in Cincinnati. Casper Klinkhammer, Henry Berger, and the Joseph Toenjes and Henry Witschen families had traveled with the Gohmanns from Cincinnati to St. Augusta.

Casper Klinkhammer also became known as Casper Klinghammer and remained a bachelor. Casper had one of the earliest known St. Augusta area land patents, September 1, 1860. He had purchased a military land warrant before departing Cincinnati. It is not known why but he boarded for a time with a family in St. Cloud and was listed there in the 1865 census. Later census documents had him back on his homestead. He must have sold his homestead by 1880 when he was listed in the St. Augusta census; once again as a border. Casper died September 20, 1899. His obituary and burial record had differing causes of death. They respectively reported heart disease and apoplexy. He was buried two days later in St. Mary Help of Christians Cemetery.

Henry Berger married into the Gohmann family and his full story was found earlier in this book.

The first St. Augusta record of the Joseph Toenjes family was the 1857 census. He also bought a military land warrant in Cincinnati and received a land patent in 1861. Joseph and Mary Toenjes were known to have four children. Later Toenjes descendants frequently married into the Gohman family. Joseph died June 1, 1888 and was buried in St. Mary Help of Christians Cemetery.

Johann "Henry" Witschen's daughter married into the Gohmann family and their full story was found earlier in this book.

The neighboring Mescher, Willenbring, Paul, Fibbe, and Beumer families originated in Ankum or Damme and their members married into the Gohman family. Other German families such

131

as Voigt, Imholte, Lubbesmeier, Toenjes, Falke, Miller, Mund, Kiffmeier, Mueller, Rienhle, Messman, and Wolters also lived nearby. There is a strong probability that some of these families were also Ankum and Damme emigrants. A number of these families also had members that eventually married into the Gohman family.

Maria Elisabeth (Börger) Gohmann had ties to the neighboring Mescher families through her mother, Maria Engel Mescher. Neighbor Johan Heinrich Fibbe was married to her second cousin, Maria Agnes Börger.

A Mund daughter married into the Gohmann family and her full story was found earlier in this book.

While in Cincinnati, neighbors, Heinrich Anton Imholte and Johan Heinrich Fibbe, had joined a settlement society. As members, they made a scouting trip to the St. Augusta area of the Minnesota Territory. After returning to Cincinnati and reporting, they returned to St. Augusta with their families. They were among the earliest to make claims on land in the area. As near as can be determined, they arrived May 1855. Johan's daughter, Maria Philomina Fibbe, was the first homestead child born in the area, April 9, 1856.

Most of these families had claimed their land under one or more of the federal homestead acts. The 1862 Homestead Act, Emancipation Proclamation and the Railroad Act were all passed at the same time and worked together to move emigrants to the west for settlement. Through their hard work, these Minnesota homesteaders became valuable agricultural producers and Central Minnesota became an important part of the nation's agriculture production. They were commonly known as being independent and "hard headed" or stubborn. They had formed a community of individuals with strong values and a sense of personal responsibility.

Family Heirlooms

By definition an heirloom is a valuable object passed down from generation to generation within a family or estate. True heirlooms were even governed by early English law. The value of the object does not necessarily have to be monetary but also can be otherwise intrinsic to the family.

A number of special heirlooms exist and continue to be cherished and handed down from generation to generation of the Gohman family.

One heirloom is an object that was given by Johann Diedrich Gohmann, the family patriarch, to Maria Elisabeth Börger, the matriarch, on their 1845 wedding day. It was used to keep the family's clothing fresh and presentable. In 1880, the brush was handed down to second generation John Diedrich Gohman. In 1904, it was passed to third generation John Diedrich Gohman. In 1935, the brush was given to fourth generation Leslie Gohman. In 1964, it was passed to the current protector of the brush, fifth generation Gary Gohman. The brush was uniquely made using various colored bristles that spell out the year of the Matriarch and Patriarch marriage. The handle of the brush has been painted with each year the brush was transferred to a later generation.

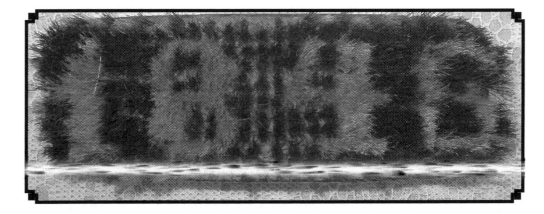

Clothes brush belonging to the Family patriarch and matriarch

Another heirloom is a muzzle loading musket that was used and cherished by Henry Berger, the spouse of the second generation Anna Marie Agnes Gohmann. Henry gave the musket to his oldest son, third generation John Dietrich Berger. He passed it on his son, fourth generation Herman Berger. When Herman died, his wife, Mildred "Minnie" made her son, fifth generation Mark Stone and current caretaker of this special heirloom. Unfortunately, the musket is missing the tamper which is the rod used to tamp the powder down the barrel of the gun.

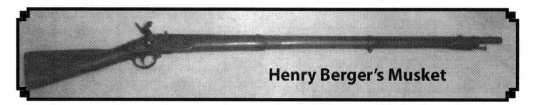

Musket belonging to second generation spouse, Henry Berger

Katherine (Mund) Gohmann's bible is another family heirloom and also contains an early family chronical. The German bible has been in the trust of the Imholte family. It was handed down to Rose Mary (Gohman) Woebkenberg, then to Mary Agnes (Woebkenberg) Imholte, and is now cared for by Mitch Imholte. The combination of the original bible and the surviving family chronical makes this a very special heirloom. The family chronical provides valuable detail about the Gohman family as a whole. The chronical starts with three pages of Katherine's German script and an additional page inserted by Rose Mary. The Imholte family care of this treasure is a gift to all. The chronical starts with information about second generation Barney Gohmann and ends with a final entry made in 1950. The bible and the first page of the chronical is depicted here.

 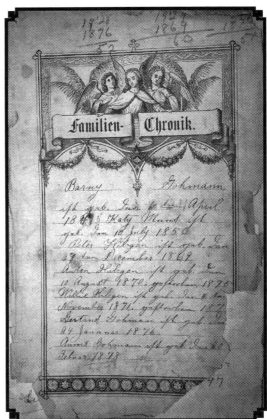

Bible and chronical belonging to second generation spouse, Katherine Mund

Most of the Gohman families maintained a "Familien Chronik" or list of major events in the family. Typically, those lists were kept in the family bible. Several of the early chronicles have been cherished and maintained to this day.

At some point Anna Maria Elisabeth (Gohmann) Gambrino created a list of important family events. Written in German, it is likely that she took some of the information from a bible belonging to the family Matriarch and Patriarch. A search for that bible has been unsuccessful. A grandson, Bernard Gambrino, has had the original list transcribed into English. Sr. Mechtilde Schmieg, O.S.B. did the translation in 1978. Two of six original pages are shown here.

Chronical belonging to second generation Anna Maria Elisabeth Gohmann

Joseph Gohmann started a list of important family events after he married Rosa in 1887. He added entries for each successive birth or death. Joseph's last entry was the marriage of his daughter, Mary Elisabeth to John Peter Machtemes in 1911. The document was written in pencil, as were letters that he is known to have written. Originally, the list was likely kept in the family bible. A great-grandson has translated the list into English.

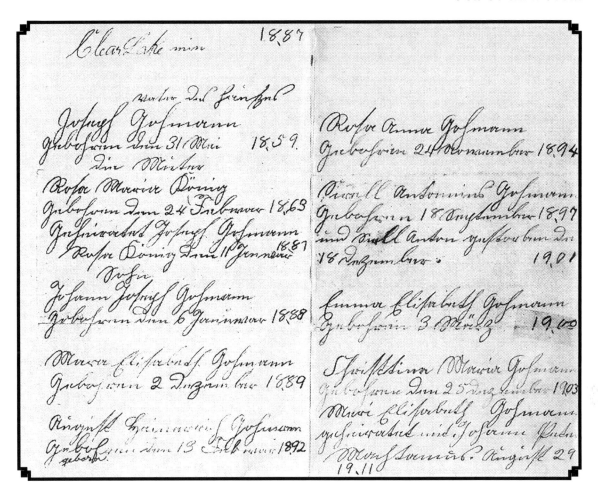

Chronical belonging to second generation Joseph Gohmann

There are several first generation and a surprising number of second generation heirloom photographs in the possession of descendants of the family patriarch, Johann Diedrich Gohmann, and the family matriarch, Maria Elisabeth Börger. These are to be cherished and protected for the enjoyment of future generations.

APPENDIX

Finding the Gohmann Family

Where did our ancestors come from?
By Charlie Kunkel

<u>Where our ancestors came from in Germany</u>

How did our ancestors' origin in Germany, in Niedersachsen shape them and ground them? How were their German roots imprinted on their humanity, on their human gifts and courage for life? How did their Roman Catholic religious origin shape their experience of God as Creator, their experience of creation and their own abilities to shape their world and to bring forth life and handle challenges and setbacks? How did their faith in Christ, in the Church support them as people of God who were loved and saved? What did they retain of their older Saxon or Teutonic spirit?

<u>You must first find us…in Germany</u>

The Gohman Genealogy Group (GGG) joined forces to find the exact location where our ancestors came from in Germany. One of the directors of the genealogy archives at the Stearns County Museum in St. Cloud, Stearns County, Minnesota told us early on that often it is not possible to find the birth place of ancestors. He said that we might have to be satisfied with knowing the name of the province or region in Germany. His words of caution made the search a more interesting challenge.

Hanover First

Most Gohman census and church records claimed Hanover as the place of origin for our ancestors; occasionally listing Prussia or Germany. Hanover was both a city and a regional territory in Germany in the 1800s when our ancestors were giving their place of birth to census takers. Years ago a Gohman researcher traveled to the city of Hanover and discovered that the records for St. Clemens Church, the only Catholic parish in this otherwise Protestant city, were located in the cathedral archives in the city of Hildesheim. This researcher visited these archives but was unsuccessful. When Gohman Cousins GG was organized, a new effort was launched to find the Gohman records of Hanover in Hildesheim. An archivist for a fee offered to search for our Gohman ancestors' records but without any promise of success. We chose not to go this route.

The fact that Hanover was both a city and a region, at least up until contemporary times, suggested that our Gohman ancestors could have originated from any part of this large northwest region of Germany now called Niedersachsen or Lower Saxony. Hanover was the capital city of the region, now called Niedersachsen, for several hundred years. In 1866 Prussia annexed Hanover, but this only lasted for a short time. Researchers were informed that German immigrants in America tended to give to census takers or to church record keepers the name of the larger government region that they came from in Germany, not the local city or town. We learned not to depend on these census or church records as a reliable guide for the place of origin. We needed to find another way.

Luxembourg Claim

Some of our current Gohman elders remembered hearing their Gohman elders claim that they were from Luxembourg. In spite of this claim, this unlikely family memory seemed related to the shifting histories of Europe. Other genealogists searching for their own ancestors' places of origin had bumped into this same unusual claim. A GGG member found the following explanation.

During the 1800s Europeans did not always associate themselves with a politically defined area. Instead their allegiance was to strong leaders. From the House of Luxembourg came many bishops, land owners, and political leaders with leadership positions across Germany and much of Europe. Some political leaders were even "pretenders" to the House of Luxembourg. They bought into the family. Once the King of the Netherlands tried to sell off Luxembourg during bad economic times because the right of being part of the House of Luxembourg (real or imagined) was the most valuable thing that the Netherlands owned at the time. Anyway, it would not have been unusual for someone originating from within this larger area of Europe to claim that they were from Luxembourg because they had been governed by someone from the House of Luxembourg, even if for a short period of time in the past.

For some years the Netherlands dominated the area we know as Luxembourg, Belgium and parts of northwestern Germany. For some historical reason people did not think highly about the "Dutch" or belonging to them. On the other hand the idea of being a Luxembourger appealed to them. So people from various regions preferred to be called Luxembourgers. Our GGG could not rely on this Gohman family memory. We needed to find the actual place of origin.

Northwest Niedersachsen Gains Ground

A genealogist friend used Google maps and other internet sources to locate the concentration of Gohman in Germany. She found that in the 18th and 19th centuries Gohmans were concentrated in a number of small villages and towns within an area northwest of the city of Hanover in the region of Niedersachsen. These Gohman towns were very close together. Some of the towns were Mettingen, Kamen, Recke, and included Ankum. This mapping pointed to a more likely place of origin for our ancestors. Later when a GGG researcher came up with Ankum as a possible location, a mapping concentration model had created a context for some confidence that we were on the right track. See the 18th and 19th century concentration of Gohman in Niedersachsen, Germany. Another internet source indicated that most of the Catholic Gohmans were living northwest of Hanover, while the Protestant Gohmans were living mostly southwest of Hanover.

A GGG member, remembered the earlier research of Fr. David Hoying, C.PP.S concerning the origin of German immigrants in southern Ohio. Fr. Hoying is a member of the Precious Blood Congregation and has published several books about German immigration. Some of his work is available on the internet. For a time Father Hoying published a newsletter about the origins of German immigrants called "Die Deutsche Ecke" (The German Corner).

Father Hoying's research established that one of the early settlers in Mercer County, Ohio was a Gohman from Ankum. We did not know yet if this Gohman family in Mercer Co. in the 1830s was related to our ancestor, John Diedrich Gohmann who lived in Cincinnati for ten years from 1844 to 1855. Nonetheless Ankum became more important as the possible place of origin for our Gohman ancestors.

The author of this article was scheduled to be in The Netherlands on a work assignment in August of 2009. Would it be possible for the GGG to assemble enough genealogical information to make a side trip to Germany worthwhile and productive? Niedersachsen seemed to be the right area of Germany because of the 18th and 19th centuries' Gohman concentration in certain cities and also because of the record that Fr. Hoying had established that at least one Gohman family from Ankum had immigrated to southern Ohio in the 1830s. The map of a providential mission began to emerge or, just possibly, the guiding hand of our ancestors was on our shoulders.

Another GGG member knew from his earlier research that Marie Elisabeth Börger, the wife of Immigrant John Diedrich Gohman, was from the town of Damme in Niedersachsen, not far from Ankum. And Fr. Hoying confirmed that he had found records that established that this Börger family had immigrated from Damme, had lived in Minster, OH for a while and then, possibly after a typhoid fever epidemic, had moved to Cincinnati, OH. He knew that the parents of Marie Elizabeth Börger were John Bernard Börger (born 1797 in Damme; died in Minster, OH 1840) and Maria Angela Mescher (dates not available). According to Fr. Hoying, Marie Elizabeth Börger had two sisters, Marie Agnes (born November 11, 1828) and Elizabeth Bernadine (born July 21, 1834), both born in Damme, Germany and both immigrated to southern Ohio.

A GGG member remembered that the names of the parents of our immigrant ancestor were given in an obituary.

This information could be necessary in locating and identifying the records of our ancestors in Germany. The names of the parents of John Diedrich Gohman were Diedrich and Adelaide Gohman.

A GGG member remembered that he had relatives in Germany who might be able to provide some assistance. Andy and Liz W. were contacted. We learned that they lived in Niedersachsen, close to Damme and Ankum, and that they were experienced genealogy researchers. Also they were related to the Börger family of Marie Elisabeth, wife of John Diedrich Gohman, and they had completed extensive research on the history of this family for their own files. Andy and Liz were eager to help. Two days in Germany were planned, August 24 and 25, 2009.

Fr. Charlie, Andy, and Liz Woebkenberg in the
reading room of the Bischoefliches Dioezesanarchiv Osnabrueck

The first day in Niedersachsen with Andy & Liz, August 24, was spent visiting cemeteries in towns where hopefully the Gohman name could still be found. We even visited a Gohman farm where the eldest Gohman had no memories or connections to our Gohman family. At the end of the first day, tired from rushing through 8-10 cemeteries and photographing dozens of Gohman tombstones, Andy & Liz patiently explained that burial plots were not helpful in locating ancestors in Germany because graves were refurbished about every 30 years and used as new burial places. We had not visited the cemetery next to St. Nicolas Church in Ankum. In preparation for this visit, Andy & Liz had consulted with genealogists most familiar with Ankum and its surrounding areas and were told that there were no records of any Gohman living in this area between 1800 and 1850. One genealogist known as an expert of emigration from the Ankum area was no longer available for consultation because of serious health problems.

On the evening of that first day in Niedersachsen Andy & Liz explained that the only possible way of locating the records of our ancestors was access to the diocesan archives of Osnabruck. They knew that the Osnabruck archives required an appointment many weeks ahead. Counting on the blessings of providence the author called an American Crosier who had been working in Germany for many years, not knowing where he lived and whether he would be available. When we called this Crosier, he had just walked into his home, arriving back from a vacation. It turned out that he worked for the Osnabruck diocese and was a personal friend of the archives director. He told us to call back in the morning at 8:00; he would try to make contact and ask for an exception to the rules. In the morning we called and were told to show up at the gate leading to the archives in 45 minutes. We made the trip and were invited in and began searching microfilmed old German records from one parish after another.

We searched the records of many parishes in the area of Ankum but not Ankum itself because Ankum genealogists had said that no Gohman family ever lived at or emigrated from Ankum in the first half of the 19th century. With a half hour remaining in the archives and with no Gohman records found, we asked for the microfilmed records of Ankum. Three of us were peering at three separate screens. Quietly behind Andy and me, Liz was creating a list of Gohman records. At a certain point Andy sensed that the silence of Liz at work was producing surprises. Andy & I turned around and saw a smile on Liz that said the search for our Gohman ancestors had been successful. Quickly Liz completed the search of the Ankum parish records. Andy made copies of each record. We paid the staff person the appropriate stipend and left totally amazed. On the way home we visited Ankum briefly. Then Andy & Liz provided a marvelous dinner feast. That evening we sent an email to the GGG, *"Wir waren erfolgreich. We were successful. We have found both of our ancestors, John Diedrich Gohman and Marie Elizabeth Borger. We have the church records for both. Our patriarch was baptized in the Church of St. Nicholas in Ankum in the Diocese of Osnabruck.. Our matriarch was baptized in the Church of St. Victor in Damme in the Diocese of Munster. These two town are about 15 miles apart. The records will be coming home with me."*

Success!

Other Research and Thoughts
— Charlie Kunkel

Gohman Family Stories and Traditions versus historic records

Family memory is an important resource for family history. Family memory preserves important elements of the actual story but not the whole story. Family memory always has to be tested against actual records if they can be found. Fortunately original records were found to provide sufficient evidence about the actual immigration story of Diedrich Gohman and his port of arrival. What remains a mystery is the identity of the other man or friend who traveled to the United States with Diedrich that was mentioned in family stories.

The originals of most historical records require some flexibility in interpreting the details of the record. For instance, an ancestor's surname and given name can be spelled in various ways on original records. The spelling of the surname, Gohman, can be found as Gohman, Gohmann, Goeman, Goman, Gomann and other versions. Also the given name of Diedrich can appear as Johann Diedrich, Johan Diedrich, Dietrick, Dederich and other versions. Also the birth date and age of an ancestor can differ on various records. What is finally important is that family memory and original records need to establish reasonable certainty that the right ancestor is being connected to the right set of memories and facts.

The Gohman Family Origins

Much of the German information concerning the Gohman family was established by the records of St. Nicolaus Catholic Church in Ankum which are stored in the archives of the Catholic Diocese of Osnabrück.

According to church records all members of Dirk Gohmann's family were from the Tütingen area, immediately south of Ankum. Another set of Gohman records were found in the Osnabruck

147

archives for Ankum, but these Gohmans were from the Loxten area, a farming area immediately north of Ankum. There was no evidence that these other Gohmans were connected to Dirk Gohmann's family in any way.

A search was conducted to find where Dirk Gohmann lived before he moved to Ankum. Church records for communities surrounding Ankum were searched, including Fürstenau, Bersenbrück, Votlage, Neuenkirchen, Bramsche, Lage and others. No birth record for Dirk Gohmann was found.

One clue about the origin of Dirk Gohmann was found in the Ankum records. It was the death record for another Dirk Gohmann who died in Ankum on March 11, 1809. His full name would have been the same as the name for Dirk Gohmann and Diedrich Gohman. He was 80 years old at his death and he was a widower. The record stated that he came from Paddenberge, which today is called Badbergen, and which is about 8 miles north of Ankum. This older Dirk Gohmann could have been the father of Dirk Gohmann, the father of Diedrich Gohman. However further research of church records from the Badbergen and nearby Quakenbruck area would have to be done to confirm this fact.

Two separate historical realities have made this research problematic. First, in earlier times the Roman Catholic churches of the Badbergen and Quakenbruck area became Lutheran because of the rule that whatever was the religion of the Prince, who controlled the area, became the official religion of all subjects who lived in that same area. A Lutheran Prince took control of this area. As a result the church records may have been moved from one location to another. Secondly, all records from Badbergen and Quakenbruck from 1687 to 1788 have been lost. One explanation was fire. Another explanation was the plundering of all churches in this area by the Swedish army during a war in the early 1700s.

This older Dirk Gohmann, who died in Ankum in 1809, was 80 years old at his death, indicating that he was born about 1729. His records and his family's church records most likely would have been part of these lost church records. Nonetheless in order to locate these family records, the records of 30 microfiche collections from this area were researched with no results.

But this older Dirk Gohmann died in Ankum at a time when the younger Dirk Gohmann lived there. Also they had the same full official name and the same commonly used name. He could have been the father of Dirk Gohmann, but it cannot be proven.

What has been established for sure is that Dirk Gohmann and his family lived in the Ankum area from 1793 until 1846 for a total of 53 years, which genealogically is a relatively brief time, that he married twice, that he had a total of nine children from the two marriages, and that by 1846 all members of this Gohman family had either died in Ankum or immigrated to the United States. There were no Gohmans in Ankum before the early 1790s or after 1846.

Gohman Family as Heuerlinger

Heuerlinger were farm workers but they never owned their own farm property. This social class of people expanded greatly over time because of a growing agricultural population and a relatively fixed number of farms. The Heuerling tradition existed at least from 1650 on. Often church records indicated what class of people an individual belonged to, when this person was being baptized, married or buried. In Germany the Lutheran churches began keeping records in 1540. Catholic churches began in 1563. During the Thirty Years War from 1618 to 1648 many church records in Germany were destroyed. But by 1650 the keeping of church records was the common practice for most churches.

At times a Heuerling family moved from one farming area to another in order to improve their economic situation or to resolve some social difficulty. The Gohman family could have moved to Ankum for some of these reasons. Maybe the farm for which they had been working elsewhere got so big that they had no time to take care of their own needs. Heuerling worked for the Boss, the Colon, whenever the Boss needed them, day and night and every day of the week. If the Heuerling had some time left over, they could work in their own small garden adjacent to their living quarters. If the living and working conditions got so bad that the Heuerling family could not survive where they were, they might choose to move on. When Heuerling had to move on for whatever reason, they had to find another farm where they would be needed and accepted as Heuerling. It was very difficult for a Heuerling to escape from this social and economic class of people.

It was also possible that in a previous location and in an earlier generation this Gohman family were property owners. Inheritance laws in that period of history required that only one member of a family inherited a farm. In some places like Damme, a neighboring city to Ankum, the oldest child inherited everything. In other places like Ankum the youngest child inherited everything. This meant that the other children got nothing. Lots of adult children from property owning farm families had to move out. Often they became Heuerling servants or farmhands because farm work was what they knew. Over centuries and generations this pattern of inheritance continued to generate a larger and larger number of Heuerling.

Sometimes if a particular farm had an extra Heuerling house available, then one or more adult children, who were inheriting nothing, could remain for a time, but only as an Heuerling. Usually farms could not provide a living for other family members for very long. Another custom allowed the previous owner, known as the Colon, who became too old or sick to manage his farm, to remain on the farm in a separate house. This custom of a separate house for the ex-Colon was called "Auf das Altenteilsetzen" ("sitting on the older part").

Another social class that provided jobs existed at this time. Someone could be trained for a certain job like carpentry, first by serving as an apprentice, then as a journeyman and finally as a master carpenter. It is reasonably certain that our Gohman ancestors in earlier generations before their arrival in Ankum did not participate in this trained labor market. The reason was, once someone was a trained laborer, he would not step down the social and work ladder to become a Heuerling. Of course tragedies and rare circumstances could happen with certain families or individuals.

Börger Family as Heuerlinger

Some records indicated that some Börger family members worked as Heuerling for a Grever family who owned a farm in Ihlendorf. But it has not been established if this Börger family was connected to the Börger family of Elisabeth.

A relative of Elisabeth Börger's family, who lives in Germany, has researched the records for Elisabeth's family and has traced its ancestry back to 1675. During the entire history from 1675 to the 1840s the Börger family lived in the area of Damme, including neighboring villages of Ihlendorf, Sierhausen, Ossenbeck and Osterdamme, all of which are only a few miles from the city of Damme. It appears that the Börger family experienced relative stability for a number of generations in the Damme area.

Immigration and Sea Passage

When members of the Gohman and Börger families decided to immigrate to the United States, they were motivated by a dream. That dream made them daring enough to cross vast waters and ride the waves of unfathomable change. In making preparations for this trip they had to deal with many challenges.

Preparations for immigration

As Heuerlinger the Gohman and Börger families belonged to the working poor with little opportunity to save for the basic expenses of transatlantic and cross country travel. The average cost per emigrant passenger from Bremen to their destination in the United States is unknown. Nonetheless it was very difficult for most Heuerling to save enough Thalers (the currency of Germany in the 19th century) to cover all their costs. To make up any shortfall, they had to negotiate a contract with a travel agent or shipping company to pay the balance after they arrived. New immigrants were bound by these contracts and could not take up their dream until they had paid them off. It is likely that this was one of the reasons Diedrich Gohman spent eleven years in Cincinnati, Hamilton County, Ohio before he moved on and pursued his dream.

The Gohman and Börger family members could never expect to make a return trip to their homeland in Germany. Immigration meant "letting go" of the past. It was both a great sacrifice and a liberation for the sake of their dream. Local government officials were even known to have

150

slammed the door shut to their homeland by warning emigrants that they would not be welcomed back if their plans to live in the United States failed.

After Napoleon was defeated in 1815, a German Confederation was established. The Constitution of this Confederation guaranteed that citizens of all German states and regions had the freedom of movement, including immigration to other countries. However Germans could not simply pack up and leave. They were required to seek release from citizenship in their homeland. This practice helped officials to identify those who might be leaving with unfulfilled military or other obligations.

Passports were needed. Emigrants got passports from a government agency. Registration lists were compiled for all who had paid their emigration bill in advance. If the name of an immigrant did not appear on a registry, it might mean that that person tried to travel as a stowaway. Sometimes stowaways, when found, were thrown overboard. They were not registered and so they simply disappeared. Sometimes so many people were leaving an area that officials decided not to create a complete list because it was too cumbersome, too much writing.

Sometimes emigrants traveled in large groups, sometimes as individuals. Churches were often involved in helping emigrants to get organized at home and then to get connected with members of their own faith community after they reached their destination. It was a great comfort for friends to travel together, to share memories, fears and plans for the future.

It is possible that the immigration to the United States and then to Cincinnati, Hamilton County, Ohio of both the Börger and Gohman families was motivated by a courtship of Elisabeth and Diedrich. In 1844 Diedrich was 30 years old and Elisabeth was 19 years old. A young man from Ankum and a young woman from Damme could have met and shared their dreams of freedom from the Heuerling lifestyle. The immigration of others had opened the door to the real possibility of transforming their dreams into reality.

Hopes and Fears of Sea Passage

German emigrants did not know the sea; they had been land locked; their dreams were mixed with fears. For weeks emigrants lived on ship below tourist class in what was called steerage, often treated as emigrant freight along with other cargo loaded together on board in the lower deck.

Usually each day emigrants got a bowl of soup. What money emigrants had was sewn into their clothes which they wore; pick-pockets were always around. Emigrants shared their dreams and fears with a small group on board, with others from the same villages or farming areas or relatives.

The fear was always present that they could be lost at sea, the ship burned up, never to be seen or heard from again. Special immigrant joy for the first sight of land would have been mixed with fear of what will happen once they arrive. Immigrants landed on the shores of large cities. Most immigrants were farmers, country folk, which would have presented another reason for fear. They wondered what would happen to them on land; how would they be accepted or rejected; how would they be able to pay for the next part of their journey.

Sickness was always a threat on board for immigrants; they wondered whether sickness would prevent them from being accepted by the authorities on land or would they be rejected because of an illness and sent back home. Immigrants during their sea passage were always seized with a mixture of dreams and of fears, living life intensely and on the move.

Life in Cincinnati

A large population of German immigrants initially settled in the Cincinnati area who used some variation of the Gohman name. Some Gohmanns were known to have lived in Cincinnati prior to 1836. The immigrants even included several other Johann Diedrich Gohmann and Johann Heinrich Gohmann families. There were even other immigrants with the names Maria Elisabeth and Maria Catherine Gohmann. The Cincinnati church records have many examples of events relative to the other Gohmanns. As an example, a Johann Bernard Gohmann got married in the old St. Mary's Catholic Church in 1856. He died in 1888, leaving a detailed will. Also there were several families named Homann or Hohmann in Cincinnati. They had similar names and birthdates as the Diedrich Gohmann family members. To add to the confusion when researching church and public record indexes, it was discovered that Diedrich and his family were often transcribed to the index as Hohmann.

German Origins

While there are no known records that indicate where Dirk Gohmann originated from, there are places worthy of more exploration. They are the town of Bersenbrück and the town of Paddenberge (now Badbergen). The towns are near each other and are north of Ankum between Oldenburg and Osnabrück. A substantial population of Gohmanns are known to have lived there since 1666, including several generations of males with names Dirk and Diedrick.

Börger Origins

One result of the Börgers living in the Damme area for such a long time was the many family groups with similar names and ages living across the area; including both the Colons, the land owners, and Heuerling, the serf class. As a result, it is often uncertain which family or individual is identified in local event records, resulting in uncertain or conflicting evidence about events. One particular situation involved a first cousin of Marie Elisabeth Börger's father, Johan Bernard Börger. The first cousin, Johan Heinrich Börger lived on a nearby Damme farm with his wife and two daughters, Maria Elisabeth and Maria Agatha, who had the same names and close ages as Elisabeth and her sister. The two Elisabeth's were born only eleven days apart. There is at least one record that also has the first cousin's wife using the same name as Elisabeth's mother! That family immigrated to Cincinnati in 1849 and is well documented. A daughter, Maria Agnes (Börger) Fibbe ended up near the Gohmanns in St. Augusta, Minnesota Territory.

Gohmanns in Ohio

Gerhard Heinrich Gohman and family's eventual destination was Minster, Auglaize County, Ohio. After he died, his wife, Wilhelmina Catherine Josepha Rehe remarried to N.G. Norman.

The groom may have also been known as Heinrich Wormann. During the ensuing years, there were apparently several marriages between Gohmanns, Wormanns, and Hohmanns. To add to the confusion, local records sometimes used the three surnames interchangeably and didn't always spell them correctly.

Börgers in Ohio

After John H. Fibbe married Maria Agnes Börger and moved to St. Augusta in the Minnesota Territory at least one other couple with the same names remained in Cincinnati. That couple, John H. and Maria Agnes (Börger) Fibbe is listed in the 1860 Cincinnati census and several other records. Another Maria Agnes Börger married a Gott in 1851 and died shortly thereafter.

Another John Bernard Börger died December 15, 1849.

Homestead Life – Early Years

Even though the early homesteaders in the St. Augusta area had not received final land patents for claimed land, it was routinely sold and traded. This often causes great confusion when researching ownership of the land. As an example, the patent of Johann Diedrich Gohmann's claimed land was signed November 20, 1864. Yet, in 1862, he sold the southernmost forty acres to Bernard Heinrich Dingmann and his wife.

Anna Marie (Gohman) and Henry Herman Berger

There are no records available to show where the Börger/Berger brothers, Henry and Gerhard, originated from in Germany. Their mother was born in Bredenborn which is part of Marienmünster, North Rhine-Westphalia, Germany. They may have come from there. Their mother had an unusually lengthy name, Maria Magdalena Anna Angela Elisabeth Nüssen. She used the nickname of Lonnie. When Henry and Gerhard's grandmother, Maria Anna Nüssen, married Georgio Ilbrecht, she kept her maiden surname. There was a German practice that the family would use the name of whichever spouse had inherited major property, usually a large family farm.

Mitchell's History of Stearns County, Volume 2 has single mention of a Captain Berger in command of three companies of troops during the Indian Uprising. That Captain Berger is not mentioned again in Mitchell's other sections about the First Regiment. The Captain is not mentioned in any other historical records including the roster of First Regiment volunteers. No records connecting this reported Berger and Henry have ever been found.

Anna Maria Elizabeth (Gohmann) and Angelo Gambrino

The picture shown in the first volume of "Our Gohman Story" and at the start of the relevant chapter in this volume is commonly accepted by the Gohman family as Anna Maria Elizabeth

(Gohmann) and Angelo Gambrino. However, the photo album created by third generation Mary Elisabeth (Gohman) Machtemes includes a notation on an original of the picture that the individuals <u>are her father, Joseph Gohman</u>, and his sister, Anna Maria Gohmann. In an attempt to determine who the correct male is, several pictures of both Angelo/Anton and Joseph were matched against the male figure in the picture in question. Images of both individuals that showed them as graying and middle aged provided amazing results; Angelo/Anton and Joseph appeared so similar that they could be taken for twins! It is much more likely that a husband and wife rather than a brother and sister would have such a formal portrait taken, especially at the age of the individuals on the picture. For that reason, the Anna Maria Elizabeth (Gohmann) and Angelo Gambrino identification is accepted and the picture used in the context of the story.

Cover

Many family members think that the ghost image of the couple emerging from the Mississippi river on the back cover is Diedrich and Gertrud Gohman. However, there is no evidence to support that opinion. There is strong evidence that the photography studio that took the original photo did not come into existence until five years after the death of Diedrich. There is also evidence that the original picture is of Henry Dirks (Dircks) & Elizabeth Holdheide. They are relatives through the Witschen family.

Cincinnati Locations

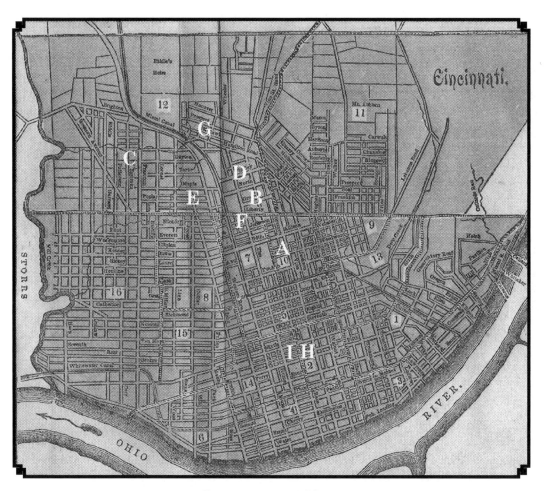

Cincinnati circa 1856 map

1. Old St. Mary Catholic Church - 123 East 13th Street

2. St. John the Baptist Catholic Church - between Bremen and Greene Streets

3. St Augustine Catholic Church - 923 Bank Street

4. Findlay Market – between Race and Elm Streets

5. Home of John Diedrich Gohmann - west row home between Ash and Maple Streets (1851-1852)

6. Home of John Diedrich Gohmann – 132 Liberty Street (1853)
   Home of John Henry Gohmann – 122 Pleasant Street (1853)

7. Home of John Henry Gohmann - 84 Mohawk Street (between 1856 and 1857)

8. Home of John Henry Gohmann - 522 Vine Street (1857)

9. Home of John Henry Gohmann's son, John Henry Gohmann - 448 Race Street (1864)

Gohmans and the Land

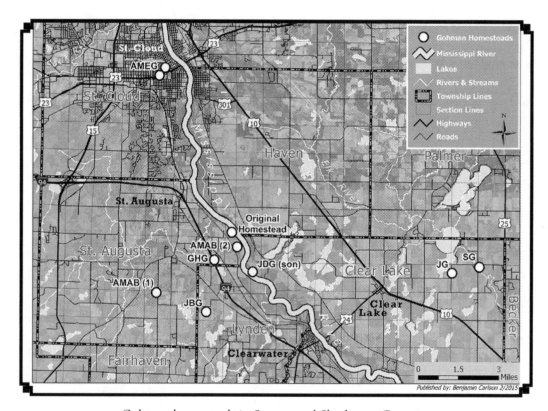

Gohman homesteads in Stearns and Sherburne Counties

Overview Explanation of Gohman Homesteads in Stearns & Sherburne Counties, Minnesota

Original Homestead: Principal homestead of John Diedrich & Elisabeth (Börger) Gohman, settled in 1856. Later, this farm became the first home of the John Diedrich & Mary (Gahr) Gohman family from 1879 until they moved across the river around 1902.

JBG: Second and principal homestead of John Bernard "Barney" & Katherine "Kate" (Mund) Gohman, settled around 1876. Before settling here, Barney & Kate had settled on a farm two miles to the north, which they soon sold to Barney's younger brother George Heinrich in 1875. Supposedly, they also purchased 16 acres from Kate's father William Mund in 1875. It is likely, then, that they would have lived there for about a year while they searched for a more permanent homestead.

AMAB (1): Homestead of Henry Herman & Anna Marie Agnes (Gohman) Berger, located in section 26 of St. Augusta Township (T123N R28W), likely settled around 1863—65. This homestead was adjacent to the homestead of Henry's brother, Gerhard Berger. By 1880, Henry Berger had sold all but 40 acres of this farm.

AMAB (2): Homestead of Henry Herman & Anna Marie Agnes (Gohman) Berger, located in section 17 of St. Augusta Township (T123N R27W). This homestead was adjacent to, and originally part of, the original homestead of John Diedrich Gohman, Anna's father. Henry Berger purchased this farm in 1867, soon after homesteading in section 26, though it is possible that he could have lived on either homestead before leaving during the civil war. The proceeds from the sale of Henry's section 26 land could have been used to purchase the section 17 farm.

GHG: Principal homestead of George Heinrich & Elisabeth (Witschen) Gohman, purchased from George Heinrich's older brother John Bernard in 1875. John Bernard originally purchased this farm in 1872. Elisabeth's step-brother, Bernard Witschen, homesteaded a farm just 1.5 miles southwest of George Heinrich and Elisabeth's home.

JDG (son): Second and principal homestead of John Diedrich & Mary (Gahr) Gohman, purchased around 1899 and settled about three years later. Before moving here, John & Mary lived across the river on the original Gohman homestead where John was born. In 1898, they mortgaged the original homestead for $2200, which was likely used to purchase their new land on the Sherburne County side of the Mississippi.

JG: Principal homestead of Joseph & Rosa (Koenig) Gohman, settled around 1880. Two of Henry & Anna Berger's sons, John Diedrich Berger & Henry Herman Berger, settled within one mile of Joseph Gohman. Elisabeth Witschen's brother, William Witschen, was also a neighbor within the one-mile radius.

AMEB: Principal homes of Angelo & Anna Maria Elizabeth (Gohman) Gambrino, in St. Cloud, Minnesota. Their first home, located at 27 16th Ave. S was their residence from 1884 until sometime before 1905, when they moved into a home at 1014 1st St. N.

SG: Principal homestead of Stephen & Catherine (Wamka) Gohman, east of Clear Lake, Minnesota. This farm was purchased in 1889 and sold in 1896 after Stephen died the previous year.

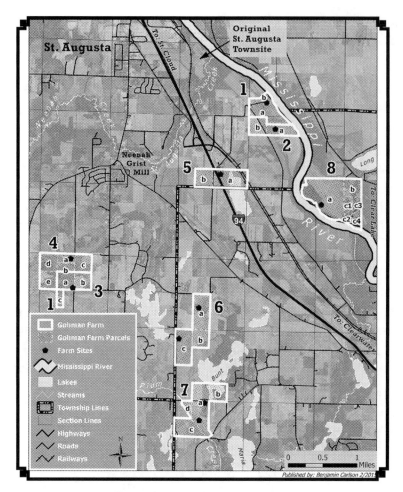

Gohman farms in the St. Augusta area

Detailed Explanation of Gohman Farm Parcels

Farm 1: Original Gohman Homestead

- October 9, 1854: John Diedrich Gohman admitted a citizen of the United States of America in Hamilton County, Ohio, allowing him to later claim his homestead under the Pre-emption Act of 1841.

- February 9, 1856: John Diedrich Gohman purchased military pension warrant No. 20082, worth 120 acres of public domain land, from a Peter Hollis, who was a private in the South Carolina Militia during the Florida War. Peter Hollis authorized John Diedrich Gohman to locate the warrant on whichever lands he chose and receive a patent for those lands. Unfortunately, it is not noted how much this transaction cost John Diedrich. Interestingly, the transaction was notarized at a court of common pleas in South Carolina.

- The Gohman family left Cincinnati on March 26, 1856, and arrived in Sauk Rapids, Minnesota several weeks later. Soon after they arrive, John Diedrich Gohman selected a location for his homestead.

- The Gohman's first temporary home was supposedly constructed on the homestead in May 1856.

- July 1 – July 7, 1856: Township 123N, Range 27W was surveyed by A.H. Runyon and four assistants. This survey was finally published April 16, 1857, allowing John Diedrich Gohman to locate his military warrant on the land that he settled in what was soon to become St. Augusta Township.

- June 26, 1860: John Diedrich Gohman applied for legal title to his land **(map parcels 1a & 2a)** using two different means: (1) he "located" his military warrant for 120 acres (purchased from Peter Hollis), and (2) he submitted a pre-proof and affidavit for his land under the Pre-emption Act of 1841.

- October 22, 1860: John Diedrich Gohman submitted an affidavit concerning the spelling of his name on his warrant application and pre-emption affidavit.

- August 6, 1862: John Diedrich Gohman sold 40 acres **(map parcel 2a)** to B.H. Dingman. John Diedrich sold this acreage before he had a title for the land, which may have caused problems as late as 1915.

- November 10, 1864: John Diedrich Gohman finally received legal title to 126.34 acres **(map parcels 1a & 2a)**, eight and a half years after he first steps foot on the land.

- Sometime between 1864 and 1879, John Diedrich Gohman acquired 17 acres near the homesteads of Henry and George Berger in Section 26 **(map parcel 1c).**

- February 1, 1879: John Diedrich Gohman the patriarch sold his farm **(map parcels 1a & 1c)** to his son John Diedrich for $1500. 40 additional acres **(map parcel 2a)** was erroneously included on the deed even though it had already been sold, which wasn't resolved until 1915.

- Sometime between 1880 and 1896, John Diedrich Gohman (son) sold the 17 acres in Section 26 **(map parcel 1c)** to T. Moeller.

- Also, an 1880 plat map shows John Diedrich Gohman had acquired 14 acres from Henry Berger's section 26 homestead **(map parcel 4b)**. By 1896, this was back in Henry Berger's name.

- Between 1896 and 1898, John Diedrich Gohman purchased 2.96 acres adjacent to the original homestead **(map parcel 1b)**, likely from neighbor Henry Fibbe.

- December 30, 1898: John Diedrich Gohman placed a mortgage on his farm and a new farm across the river (map parcels 1a, 1b, & 8a), likely to finance the purchase of his future home. The mortgage was paid off by April 5, 1902.

- March 25, 1902: John Diedrich Gohman sold the original homestead to Anna T. Kiffmeyer (map parcels 1a & 1b) for $2600

- The Gohman farm remained in the Kiffmeyer family until August 16, 1950, when it was sold to Norbert & Valeria Gohman. The farm (map parcels 1a, 1b, 2a, 2b) is currently owned by their sons Lloyd and Leroy Gohman.

Farm 2: Section 17 homestead of Henry and Anna (Gohman) Berger

- September 6, 1862: BH Dingman purchased 40 acres (map parcel 2a) from John Diedrich Gohman for $250. For the history of this parcel before 1862, refer to farm 1.

- May 6, 1867: BH Dingman sold 40 acres (map parcel 2a) to Henry Herman Berger for $500.

- Between 1867 and 1880, Henry Berger acquired 40 acres adjacent to his farm (map parcel 2b).

- Henry Berger died in 1893, but his land remained in his estate until at least 1896. By 1912 it was owned by his children, who then sold it to Ida and Harry Young sometime before 1914.

- February 20, 1914: Henry Berger (son of Henry Herman) purchased the 80 acre homestead (map parcel 2a & 2b) back from Ida and Harry Young for $2400.

- February 25, 1915: John Diedrich Gohman gave a deed to his nephew Henry Berger for 40 acres (map parcel 2a) in order to clear the title of said property, since John Diedrich the patriarch mistakingly included this parcel in the deed when he sold the farm to his son in 1879.

- Sometime between 1915 and 1923, Henry Berger sold the homestead (map parcel 2a & 2b) to Julius and Augusta Stuewe, who in turn sold the farm to C.D. Schwab on August 24th 1923.

- Between 1929 and 1946, the Berger homestead (map parcel 2a & 2b) was owned in turn by the Minnesota Finance Company, J.B. Storkamp, the State of Minnesota, and finally B.H. Kiffmeyer, who owned the original Gohman homestead to the North.

- On August 16, 1950, B.H. Kiffmeyer sold both the Gohman and Berger homesteads to Norbert & Valeria Gohman. The farm **(map parcels 1a, 1b, 2a, 2b)** is currently owned by their sons Lloyd and Leroy Gohman.

Farm 3: George Berger homestead

- 1856: George H. Berger arrived in Stearns County, Minnesota, and proceeded to settle in what would soon be section 26 of St. Augusta Township.

- July 1, 1861: George Berger purchased and received a patent title for his 40 acres homestead **(map parcel 3a)** from the U.S. Government.

- Between 1861 and 1873, George purchased 40 acres adjacent to his homestead **(map parcel 3b)**, as well as 40 acres from his brother Henry Berger **(map parcel 2c)**, bringing his farm to 120 acres.

- George died in 1873, but his farm remained in the family until at least 1880. Soon after that, his wife Mary remarried and his 40 acre homestead was sold to G.W. Knettle **(map parcel 3a)**, and his other 80 acres to Mabel S. Griffith **(map parcels 3b & 2c)**.

Farm 4: Section 26 homestead of Henry and Anna (Gohman) Berger

- Before 1865: Henry Herman Berger settled in Section 26 of St. Augusta Township near his brother George's homestead.

- May 15, 1867: Henry Herman Berger married Anna Marie Gohman.

- September 1, 1868: Henry and Anna Berger received a homestead patent for 160 acres **(map parcels 4a—4e)** in Section 26 after applying through the Homestead Act of 1862.

- Between 1868 and 1880, Henry Berger sold 40 acres each to neighbors H. Krebs **(map parcel 4d)** and J.J. Kronenberger **(map parcel 4e)**, as well as his brother George **(map parcel 4c)**. The money from these land sales was ostensibly used to purchase a second homestead **(map parcels 2a & 2b)**.

- An 1880 plat map also shows that Henry Berger had sold 14 acres to his brother-in-law John Diedrich Gohman **(map parcel 4b)**. By 1896, this land was back in Henry Berger's name.

- Henry Berger died in 1893, but his land remained in his estate until at least 1896. By 1912 it was owned by his children.

- February 3, 1913: The children of Henry Berger, who owned the remainder of his estate in common, sold the last 40 acres of the original homestead **(map parcel 4a & 4b)** to Anton & Gertrude Schill for $800.

- June 11, 1918: Anton Schill sold 40 acres (map parcels 4a & 4b) to John L. Kiffmeyer for $1000, in whose family it remains to this day.

Farm 5: Homestead of George Heinrich & Elisabeth (Witschen) Gohman

- October 1, 1872: John Bernard Gohman purchased 80 acres **(map parcel 5a)** from Henry & Mary Schlagbeck for $475.

- April 5, 1875: John Bernard Gohman sold 80 acres **(map parcel 5a)** to his younger brother, George Heinrich Gohman, for $500.

- January 3 1881: George Heinrich Gohman purchased 40 additional acres **(map parcel 5b)** from Henry Beumer for $320.

- June 29, 1882: The Minneapolis & Northwestern Railroad (later the Great Northern Railway) purchased a 100 foot wide perpetual railroad easement for $175.

- George Heinrich Gohman died on March 31st, 1904. His wife Elisabeth died on August 16, 1907.

- April 6, 1908: Bernard H. Gohman (son of George Heinrich & Elisabeth) purchased 120 acres **(map parcels 5a, 5b & 7d)** along with another farm (refer to farm 7, parcel c) from the estate of Elisabeth Gohman (administered by Henry Gohman) for $3500.

- May 14, 1908: Bernard H. Gohman sold his father's homestead **(map parcels 5a, 5b & 7d)** to his brother John Henry Gohman for $2500.

- May 6, 1965: John Henry & Josephine Gohman pass on their farm **(map parcels 5a & 5b)** to their son Ernest.

- October 5, 1967: 11 acres is purchased for the right-of-way for Interstate 94.

- August 11, 1986: John M. Schwinghammer purchased all of the farm east of I-94. This part of the farm was later acquired by John's brother Donald, then the City of St. Cloud. Today, the farm is empty, having been razed around 2005.

- May 9, 1988: Lloyd & Leroy Gohman purchased all of the farm west of I-94. This part of the farm is still owned by them to this day.

Farm 6: Homestead of John Bernard "Barney" & Katherine (Mund) Gohman

- Barney Gohman sold his first farm to his brother George Heinrich on April 5th, 1975.

- Following this sale, Barney & Kate purchased sixteen acres from Kate's father in May 1875. It is not known how long they owned this land, but they sold it before 1880.

- Around 1876, Barney and Kate likely began a new homestead in Lynden Township.

- July 20, 1881: Barney Gohman received a homestead patent for their 80 acre homestead **(map parcel 6a)** through the Homestead Act of 1862.

- Sometime between 1880 and 1896, Barney Gohman acquired 80 acres adjacent to his homestead **(map parcel 6c)**. Between 1896 and 1910, he had sold this land to Clements and Mary (Gohman) Pothoff, daughter and son-in-law of George Henry and Elisabeth Gohman. This farm remained in the Pothoff family until the 1930's, when it was sold to Stephen & Anna Toenjes.

- December 10, 1908: Barney Gohman purchased an additional 40 acres **(map parcel 6b)** from the Great Northern Railway Company for $320.

- September 17, 1910: Barney & Kate Gohman sold 120 acres **(map parcels 6a & 6b)** to their son Christopher "Christ" Gohman for $3000.

- Sometime between 1925 and 1947, Christ Gohman sold the homestead **(map parcels 6a & 6b)** to William H. & Alma Zipp. Today, it is owned by Joann Hagen, etal.

Farm 7: Additional lands acquired by John Bernard & George Heinrich Gohman

- Sometime between 1880 and 1896, John Bernard Gohman acquired 80 acres 1 mile south of his homestead **(map parcel 7a)**.

- Sometime between 1896 and 1908, John Bernard Gohman had sold this 80 acres **(map parcel 7a)** to his brother George Heinrich.

- Also, sometime between 1896 and 1880, George Heinrich Gohman acquired 81.75 acres adjacent to this land from G.W. Newell **(map parcel 7c)** and another parcel along Plum Creek from George Warner **(map parcel 7d)**.

- April 6, 1908: Bernard H. Gohman (son of George Heinrich & Elisabeth) purchased two of these parcels **(map parcels 7c & 7d)** along with the George Heinrich Gohman homestead from the estate of Elisabeth Gohman (administered by Henry Gohman) for $3500.

- April 10, 1908: John D. Gohman (oldest son of George Heinrich & Elisabeth) purchased 80 acres **(map parcels 7a)** from the estate of Elisabeth Gohman (administered by Henry Gohman) for $1475. Between 1908 and 1912, John D. acquired 40 more acres adjacent to this **(map parcel 7b)**, possibly from the Great Northern Railway Company.

- May 14, 1908: Bernard H. Gohman sold his father's homestead, along with the Plum Creek parcel (**map parcels 5a, 5b & 7d**) to his brother John Henry Gohman for $2500, yet he continued to farm on the other parcel he acquired (**map parcel 7c**) for many years.

- Between 1912 and 1925, John Henry Gohman had sold the small Plum Creek parcel (**map parcel 7d**) to John Hinkemeyer.

- Over the years, the John D. Gohman and Bernard H. Gohman farms have been continually farmed by the Gohman family. Today, Bernard "Bernie" Gohman and his son Bradley still farm much of these two farms (**map parcels 7a—7c**).

Farm 8: Second homestead of John Diedrich Gohman (son)

- In 1898 John Diedrich Gohman purchased 143.54 acres of new land on the East bank of the Mississippi River (**map parcel 8a**).

- December 30, 1898: John Diedrich mortgaged his new farm and the homestead where he grew up (**map parcels 8a, 1a & 1b**) in order to pay for these new lands he purchased. The mortgage is through Charles S. Crandall for $2200 and is paid off by January 26th, 1909.

- March 25, 1902: John Diedrich Gohman sold the original homestead to Anna T. Kiffmeyer (**map parcels 1a & 1b**) for $2600.

- June 1907: John Diedrich granted the Mississippi & Rum River Boom Co. permission to drive pilings along the shore of the river on his farm for the purpose of facilitating log drives.

- December 1, 1905: John Diedrich purchased 102.75 acres on the east side of his farm (**map parcels 8b & 8c**) for $1644.

- August 1, 1910: John Diedrich's farm was condemned by the State of Minnesota so as to allow portions of it to be flooded behind a dam proposed by William A. Clark. Fortunately for the Gohman family, this dam is never constructed.

- Between 1935 and 1943, 20 acres were sold to Anthony Gohman (**map parcels 8c3-4**), and another 40 acres (**map parcel 8b**) were sold as well.

- John Diedrich died October 3, 1934. His wife Mary owned the farm until August 25, 1943, when it was purchased by their son Edward Gohman and his wife Rose (**map parcels 8a, 8c1-2**).

- Later, the farm was purchased by Don & Eulalia Gohman. Eventually, another 26.75 acres were sold off for a housing development (**map parcels 8c2-3**), but 159.54 intact acres remain in the Gohman family to this day (**map parcels 8a & 8c1**).

Farm 9: Homestead of Joseph and Rosa (Koenig) Gohman

- Around 1880, Joseph Gohman supposedly homesteaded on 120 acres in Sherburne County at the age of 21. His residence there was confirmed by the 1885 census.

- January 11, 1887: Joseph Gohman & Rosa Koenig are wed.

- By 1903, Joseph & Rosa own 160 acres **(map parcel 9a)**.

- Also, by 1903, Joseph Gohman owned 40 acres in partnership with Frank Goenner **(map parcel 9c)**. This partnership was still intact in 1914.

- Between 1903 and 1914, Joseph purchased 80 additional acres **(map parcel 9b)** from D. Woodbury.

- February 26, 1946: Joseph Gohman passed away in Clear Lake. By the 1960's, his farm **(map parcels 9a & 9b)** was owned by Donald Eilers, and by the 1980's the homestead was owned by John Gallagher **(map parcel 9a)**.

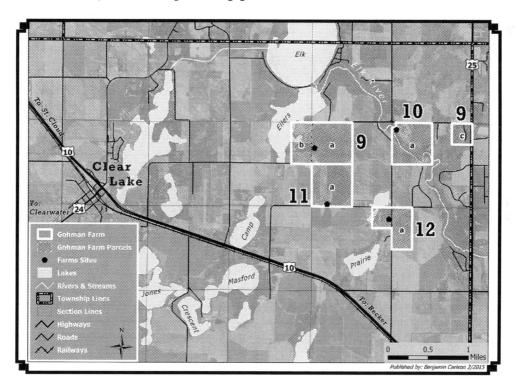

Gohman farms in the Clear Lake area

Farm 10. Homestead of Stephen & Catherine (Wamka) Gohman

- September 1, 1857: James H White purchased and received a patent title for 160 acres on the Elk River **(map parcel 10a)**. Before the title is issued, 4 acres is split off of the Northwest corner. Later, 156 acres are sold to Charles Potter.

- January 1889: Charles Potter sold 156 acres to Stephen Gohman for $1000 **(map parcel 10a)**.

- Stephen Gohman married Catherine Wamka on June 30, 1890, but he died only five years later.

- June 5, 1896: Catherine Gohman sold 156 acres to Herman Eilers for $1200 **(map parcel 10a)**.

- By 1899, Herman Eilers had sold the farm to Fredrick Eilers. The farm remains in the Eilers family to this day.

Farm 11: Homestead of Henry Herman Berger, son of Henry Herman & Anna Marie (Gohman) Berger

Farm 12: Homestead of John Diedrich Berger, son of Henry Herman & Anna Marie (Gohman) Berger

"The Third Generation" Volume **ERRATA**

This appendix addresses incorrect information contained in the first Gohman Book; "Out Gohman Story, *The Third Generation*". It includes corrections to text and formatting errors plus new information.

Table of Contents, 2ⁿᵈ page, last line (formatting error)

Page 12, Children List, item 9 and new item 11 (text and formatting error)
　　　Correction – remove item 9, renumber, and add new item 11 – Stephen Frank Gohman

Page 20, Children List, item 1 (typo)
　　　Old – Bernard Celsius Imholte (1899-1973) married Olivia Klaverkamp (1905-1967)
　　　Correction – Bernard Celsus Imholte (1899-1973) married Olivia Klaverkamp (1905-1967)

Page 38, 3ʳᵈ paragraph (incorrect text)
　　　Correction – remove 2ⁿᵈ sentence in its entirety

Page 58, 1ˢᵗ paragraph, 3ʳᵈ line (typo)
　　　Old - for $200,000.
　　　Correction - for $20,000.

Pages 71-72, entire story (new information) – change name
　　　Old - Henry John Berger
　　　Correction – Henry Herman Berger

Page 113, 4th paragraph, 4th line (incorrect text)
 Old – Machtemes, a first cousin of Elizabeth,
 Correction - Machtemes, a friend of the groom

Page 118, Children List, item 2 (new information)
 Old – Michael Joseph "Mick" Weinand (1905-1970) married Lillian Aumann (1910-)
 Correction – Michael Joseph "Mick" Weinand (1905-1970) married Lillian Aumann (1910-2013)

Page 122, Children List, item 6 (new information)
 Old – Delia Ida Arnold (1912-) married Miles Roland Nelson (1910-1989)
 Correction – Delia Ida Arnold (1912-2013) married Miles Roland Nelson (1910-1989)

Page 128, Children List, item 6 (typo)
 Old – Elizabeth Alvira Berger (1925-2006) married Frank Xavier Lamecha (1918-1996)
 Correction – Elizabeth Alvira Berger (1925-2006) married Frank Xavier Malecha (1918-1996)

Page 149, Children List, item 9 (typo)
 Old - William Moritz Beumer (1918-2007) married Pauline Kliker (1924)
 Correction - William Moritz Beumer (1918-2007) married Pauline Klinkner (1924)

Page 155, Children List, item 4 (typo)
 Old – Walter George Gohman (1914-1922) married Olivia Margaret Kramer (1919-1998)
 Correction – Walter George Gohman (1914-1992) married Olivia Margaret Kramer (1919-1998)

Page 174, Children List, item 3 (new information)
 Old – Henry Otto Frerich (1917-2008) married Phylis Maria Gronau (1924-2010)
 Correction – Henry Otto Frerich (1917-2008) married Phyllis Maria Gronau (1924-2010)

Page 187, Children List, item 6 (new information)
 Old – Juletta Hilda Gohman (1918) married Harold Joseph Klein (1917-1985)
 Correction - Juletta Hilda Gohman (1918-2013) married Harold Joseph Klein (1917-1985)

Page 197, Title (formatting error)
 Old – Maria Elizabeth Agnes Gohman
 Correction – Maria Elizabeth Agnes (Gohman) Derr

Page 217, Children List, item 8 (new information)
 Old – Hildegard Elizabeth Gohman (1931-) married Myron E. Ayer (1921-)
 Correction – Hildegard Elizabeth Gohman (1931-2013) married Myron Elmer Randall Ayer (1921-2013)

Page 238. Paragraph 2, line 2 (new information)
    Old –Sherburne County.
    Correction - Benton County.

Page 271, Children List, item 1 (new information)
    Old – Elizabeth Marie Etnier (1927-2012) married Joseph William Leach (?-)
    Correction – Elizabeth Marie Etnier (1927-2012) married Joseph William Leach (1924-2013)

Page 291, Children List, item 5 (new information)
    Old – Angelo Leo Gambrino (1929-) married Marleen L. Theissen (1929-2009)
    Correction – Angelo Leo Gambrino (1929-) married Marleen L. Theisen (1929-2009)